THE PEOPLE'S DOONESBURY

G.B. TRUDEAU

THE PEOPLE'S
DOONESBURY

NOTES FROM UNDERFOOT, 1978~1980

HOLT, RINEHART AND WINSTON · NEW YORK

Library of Congress Catalog Card Number: 81-80815
ISBN Hardbound: 0-03-049166-5
ISBN Paperback: 0-03-049171-1

Designer: Amy Hill
Printed in the United States of America

The cartoons in this book have appeared in newspapers
in the United States and abroad under the auspices of
Universal Press Syndicate.

1 3 5 7 9 10 8 6 4 2

TO THE MEMORY OF MY FRIEND
AND EDITOR, JIM ANDREWS

AN ANNOTATED CONVERSATION WITH THE AUTHOR

Publisher's Note: For the past several years, the editors of this imprint have sought to persuade cartoonist G. B. Trudeau to go on the record with some thoughts about his life and work. For a few exhilarating weeks before this volume went to press, Trudeau was believed to have been interested. His interest, however, did not blossom into actual consent, so the following interview was regrettably obtained under the false understanding it would only be published in a French film magazine.

As rich in detail as the final transcript was, certain of the artist's references cried out for clarification or addenda, and, for this reason, his remarks have been periodically annotated.

Q: Given all the opportunities you've had, why have you resisted fame these many years?

A: I'm not altogether sure. Perhaps because it requires getting out more than I'd like. If you're serious about it, nurturing a public image, unlike building a reputation, is not something you can do in the privacy of your own living room. It's not just that fame is corrupting; it's time-consuming.[1] You're always busy trying to live up to your latest version of yourself.

Q: Aren't we all?

A: Yes, but it's nice not to have to shave beforehand. Listen, some years ago I did a talk show in Boston. I was twenty-two and I'd been doing the strip for about six months. After a brief introduction, the hostess turned to me and asked what it was like to be rich, famous, and eligible. I hadn't the faintest idea what she was talking about. After staring at her in dumb panic for about five seconds, I finally just rolled my eyes. The hostess looked very pleased and cut to a commercial. I never did another television show.[2]

Q: You must have been tempted, though. I read somewhere that you and Pope John Paul are the only two people ever to have turned down an interview with "60 Minutes."

A: Well, I don't think too much should be made of that. With the Pope, there was a scheduling conflict. They tried to book him on Easter, which is pretty arrogant if you think about it. In my case, I missed the message on my answering service.[3] Unless you've been defrauding widows out of their life savings, "60 Minutes" doesn't call twice.

[1] For Trudeau, so is anonymity. He once hid in his bathroom for three hours to avoid a reporter from the *Baltimore Sun.*

[2] Not entirely true. He did appear on "To Tell the Truth," where only one of the four panelists chose him over the two impostors. Trudeau walked away with $167 and a pair of jade cufflinks.

[3] Trudeau's answering service, VIP of New Haven, played a continuing role in the cartoonist's isolation from the outside world—at least it did until a crate of original strips belonging to Trudeau was removed from its office only to be recovered in a police raid on the Sunshine Girls Escort Service in Hamden, Connecticut. Sunshine's unlucky social director was subsequently convicted of first-degree larceny, partly on the strength of Trudeau's ability to recognize his own work in court.

Q: That sounds a shade ingenuous, but let's go on. . . . You are reported to go to some lengths when you are preparing a sequence in the strip. How much research do you really do?

A: As little as I can possibly get away with. It is for this quality above all others, I think, that I am so admired by undergraduates; I know just enough to create the impression I know a lot. And, of course, being a cartoonist helps. If it weren't for the hopelessly low expectations with which people turn to my section of the newspaper, I'm sure I would have been exposed years ago.

Q: You know, if you're going to continue being self-effacing, we might as well forget the whole thing. Frankly, it's not very interesting. Don't you feel good about yourself?

A: Of course I feel good about myself. You don't think I've got reason to? What's the Pulitzer Prize, chopped liver?[4]

Q: Okay, okay. Tell us about the prize.

A: What's to tell. . . . It's the classiest award in America. No dinner, no acceptance speeches, no TV show. They just call you up and say, "Good going, the check is in the mail." Everybody in my neighborhood was very proud of me. My grocer asked me what I was going to do with the two hundred thousand dollars. I think he thought I won the Pulitzer on a quiz show.[5]

Q: Speaking of easy money, why haven't you gotten into product licensing? The annual gross of the *Peanuts* empire is said to exceed the GNP of your average emerging nation.

A: Well, Sparky Schulz simply takes the position that the spin-offs make people happy. I have no problem with that position, but with the exception of the books, I prefer to keep my characters on the reservation. Perhaps it's because there's no logical connection between my characters and a lunch box. . . unless, of course, you find the logic of the profit motive irresistible.

Q: May we assume you'd loan your characters out for charity?[6]

A: You're missing the point. It's a matter of artistic pride. I think the case against merchandising was best made by the nine-year-old boy who once wrote to inquire why I wasn't selling any *Doonesbury* "by-products."

Q: You seem to be preoccupied with the idea of purity in your work.

[4]When Trudeau, in 1975, became the first comic-strip artist to win the Pulitzer Prize for Editorial Cartooning, the Editorial Cartoonists' Society proposed a resolution condemning the Pulitzer committee. Trudeau, once assured the award was irrevocable, supported the resolution.

[5]The award was actually in the amount of $2,000. Trudeau blew most of it on household bills and some unnecessary minor surgery.

[6]The interviewer's facetiousness was unwarranted. Trudeau had in fact once used several of his characters to promote a Connecticut Red Cross blood drive.

A: Somebody has to be. If you have a good editor, as I had for ten years in Jim Andrews, you come to realize that the inner life of a comic strip is a very fragile ecosystem.[7] It has its own rules, its own time frames, its own internal logic. That logic may be completely askew, but if you tinker with it, the chances are pretty good the whole thing will collapse.

Q: Could you elaborate?

A: Yes, but I'd rather not. I only put in that last bit for people who might be working on dissertations.

Q: That's very thoughtful, but...

A: Look, E. B. White once compared the analysis of humor to dissecting a frog; that is, it can be done, but the frog tends to die in the process.

Q: Where do you see satire going in the decade ahead?

A: You're asking me to predict a trend? You must be mad. I only do postmortems.

Q: All right, where has satire been? What about "Saturday Night Live"?

A: A magnificent missed opportunity. The reason why "SNL" ultimately doesn't matter is that the show never developed a point of view. Originally, the program produced some pretty good guerrilla theater, but with its success, it quickly evolved into a smug exercise in slash-and-burn humor—anarchy for its own sake. Nothing of value was ever left standing. This was a major failing, I think, because great satire has always had some sort of moral underpinnings—just ask Richard Pryor or Lily Tomlin.

Q: Or Garry Trudeau?

A: Yes, but don't look for conviction. I'm like Don Corleone. I've got a business to run.

Q: That's how you justify cuffing people for a living?

A: Absolutely. It's my job. I'm a form of social control. I make no apologies.

Q: Perhaps you should. One of the things that troubles some people about *Doonesbury* is that it's hard to know when you're reporting and when you're making things up. For instance, did Jerry Brown really solicit a political contribution from Sidney Korshak, the alleged organized-crime figure, as you charged in one series?

[7]Andrews realized Trudeau's limitations. He once described the cartoonist as "a thoughtful, creative, and highly concerned young man who is out to make a fast buck."

[8]When asked by NBC reporter Brian Ross, who originally broke the story, why he had solicited a contribution from a man chronically under federal investigation, Brown replied, "Even Jane Fonda was once investigated by the FBI." Later, he described other charges made in the strip as "false and libelous," but declined to press the issue on the novel grounds that "the First Amendment allows libel by the press."

[9]Tom Hayden, among other disinterested observers, wrote that Trudeau's view of Brown was "bigoted."

A: Yes. Actually, Brown doesn't deny this.[8] But most California papers killed the strips on the grounds that I had trampled the rights of a man the FBI had called one of the most influential mobsters in the country. Whimsically enough, the only two papers outside of Brown's home state to share this concern were located in — you guessed it — Reno and Las Vegas.

Q: Do you know Brown personally?

A: Nope. I once met Linda, which, of course, I recognize as not being the same thing.

Q: Some of Brown's admirers charge you've been uncommonly tough on him.[9] Perhaps if you got to know him, you'd feel differently about him.

A: Exactly. Which is as good an excuse as any to pass. One of the reasons why public figures get to be public figures in the first place is that they are not without charm. Insisting, as a George Will does, that one must get in close to make those lovely, nuanced judgment calls is utter nonsense. I'm not interested in private assurances or endearments, the insider's "access." I'm interested in what the outsider sees — the public face the politician *chooses* to project, *chooses* to be judged on. Nothing could be fairer. He's setting the agenda; I'm merely reacting.

Q: You're all heart.

A: Actually, I'm all boy. If you think this business is fun, you're right....

THE ROTUNDA STRIKES BACK

Q: Is it true that Tip O'Neill tried to head off a couple of strips about him during the Korean scandal?

A: Yes, but I think he was getting bad advice. A comic strip is not one of those things you want to look too worried about. One of the strips concerned a dubious nursing-home deal the speaker had drifted into.[1] To the delight of all the papers who picked up the story, this time I actually had my facts straight.[2] The other strip was a mail-in coupon, in which it was implied that Tip was among those who had benefited from Tongsun Park's largesse. It was a shameless gimmick, of course. And since the coupon was then reprinted in all the news stories, readers were given two opportunities to cut it out and send it in.

Q: How many did O'Neill receive?

A: Nobody knows. After the tenth bag of postcards was carted over to the Speaker's office, the post office was alerted to stop delivery. Now *that's* lobbying. It was a gun nut's wet dream.

[1]Gary Hymel, the Speaker's press secretary, offered to show Trudeau cancelled checks that he claimed absolved O'Neill from any impropriety. The offer was quickly withdrawn when Trudeau suggested that their authenticity be verified by *The New York Times*.

[2]And the courage to stand behind them. The artist's long-time mentor and confidant, Nicholas von Hoffman, later commended Trudeau for having the right stuff, saying that he had upheld the highest traditions of "investigative cartooning."

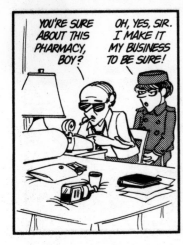

PROFESSOR KISSINGER, OL' WEINBURGER HERE'S BEEN MAKING A PRETTY STRONG CASE AGAINST GOING TO THE SHA-NA-NA'S DINNER! WHAT'S YOUR REPLY?

HEY, BARNEY..

NO, NO, IT'S ONLY FAIR! LET HIM GIVE HIS SIDE!

THANK YOU, MR. PERKINS. I'M GRATEFUL TO FINALLY HAVE A CHANCE TO PUT THE DINNER AND ITS SPONSOR IN THE PROP-ER PERSPECTIVE.. SPONSOR?

THE FRIENDS OF EXXON SOCIETY WAS FOUNDED IN..

NEVER MIND.

GOOD EVENING. THIS IS THE SCENE IN NEW YORK TONIGHT AS HUNDREDS OF DEMONSTRATORS GATHER OUTSIDE A DINNER FOR THE EMPRESS OF IRAN. ROLAND HEDLEY IS THERE.

HARRY, THERE'S BEEN A SLIGHT DELAY IN THE FESTIVITIES TONIGHT AS WE AWAIT THE LATE ARRIVAL OF PRO-SHAH FORCES HERE AT THE NEW YORK HILTON HOTEL.

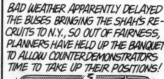

BAD WEATHER APPARENTLY DELAYED THE BUSES BRINGING THE SHAH'S RECRUITS TO N.Y., SO OUT OF FAIRNESS, PLANNERS HAVE HELD UP THE BANQUET TO ALLOW COUNTERDEMONSTRATORS TIME TO TAKE UP THEIR POSITIONS!

LONG LIVE THE SHAH!

..AND HERE THEY COME NOW! LOOKS LIKE THE EVENING'S UNDER WAY, HARRY!

HARRY, I'M TALKING TO A COUPLE OF STUDENTS RIGHT NOW, BUT UNLIKE MOST OF THE FOREIGN DEMONSTRATORS HERE, THESE YOUNG MEN ARE AS AMERICAN AS YOU OR I!

MOREOVER, I AM TOLD THAT THEY ARE STUDENTS OF DR. HENRY KISSINGER, THE FEATURED SPEAKER AT TONIGHT'S DINNER HONORING THE EMPRESS!

GENTLEMEN, TELL ME, WHY ON EARTH ARE YOU WEARING THOSE MASKS? SURELY YOU'RE NOT PROTECTING RELATIVES OR LOVED ONES IN IRAN?

NO, BUT WE'VE GOT MIDTERMS COMING UP, MAN..

WHOA! SAY NO MORE!

HEY, LOOK! IT'S SHIRLEY MACLAINE!

SHIRLEY MACLAINE? I DON'T BELIEVE IT! WHAT'S SHE DOING HERE?

HEY, SHIRL! WHAT GIVES? DON'T YOU KNOW WHAT HAPPENS TO POLITICAL DISSIDENTS IN IRAN?

FOR YOUR INFORMATION, FELLAH, IRANIAN DISSIDENTS ARE SENT TO THE SHAH'S PRISONS, WHERE THEY ARE INTERROGATED, BRUTALIZED, AND RARELY HEARD FROM AGAIN!

OH. YOU HEARD, THEN.

THAT'S RIGHT. SO YOU CAN STOP ACTING SO DAMN SUPERIOR!

OKAY, MR. DUKE, I'M ALL EARS. WHY SHOULD I HIRE YOU AS MY GENERAL MANAGER?

BECAUSE, MR. WILLIAMS, YOU'RE A MAN WITH A PROBLEM. YOU'VE TRADED AWAY ALL YOUR DRAFT CHOICES, AND ALL YOU'VE GOT LEFT IS A GANG OF ATROPHYING OLD GEEZERS!

NOW, IN A YEAR OR SO, YOUR OPTIONS WILL BE OPENING UP. BUT IN THE MEANTIME, YOU NEED SOMEONE WHO CAN KEEP THE OLD-TIMERS KEYED, CONFIDENT, AND OUT OF PAIN!

COULD YOU BE MORE SPECIFIC?

SURE! SUPPOSE, JUST SUPPOSE, YOU'VE BEEN PLAYING KILMER ON ONLY 50 MGS. DEXEDRINE, SEE?..

MR. DUKE, I THINK YOU'RE QUITE MISTAKEN ABOUT THE EXTENT OF THE PILL PROBLEM. WHY, NFL OFFICIALS GIVE ANTI-DRUG LECTURES EVERY MONTH..

YEAH, AND 90% OF YOUR PLAYERS ARE LAUGHING THEIR JOCKS OFF THE WHOLE TIME!

MR. WILLIAMS, YOUR PLAYERS AREN'T PILLHEADS BECAUSE THEY **WANT** TO BE. HELL, NOBODY **LIKES** TAKING PILLS! THEY TAKE 'EM BECAUSE THEY'RE CONCERNED ABOUT WHAT THE NEXT ATHLETE MIGHT BE DOING!

OH.. OH, I SEE.

IT'S A REAL PROBLEM, SIR! AND I'LL TELL YOU, SOMETIMES IT JUST BREAKS MY HEART TO SEE IT!

BUT YOU SAY YOU'VE HAD SOME EXPERIENCE IN THIS AREA?

I'VE BEEN AROUND THE TRACK A FEW TIMES, YES.

MR. WILLIAMS, I HOPE I'M NOT BEING OUT OF LINE IN TELLING YOU THAT I THINK I UNDERSTAND YOUR PROBLEM. BASICALLY, YOU'RE HOT FOR THE SUPER BOWL!

CAN YOU GET ME THERE, MR. DUKE?

WITH TIME? WITHOUT QUESTION, SIR! BUT I'D BE REMISS IF I FAILED TO MENTION THAT MY TALENTS ARE IN CONSIDERABLE DEMAND NOW!

WELL, DO YOU THINK YOU COULD LIVE WITH $100,000 A YEAR?

HMM.. I'D LIKE TO, SIR, I REALLY WOULD. BUT WITH MY MOTHER IN THE HOSPITAL NOW..

PITY. COULD YOU SUGGEST ANYONE ELSE WHO..

OH, THE HECK WITH MOM! THIS IS TOO IMPORTANT!

"..AND WE IN THE FRONT OFFICE OFFER MR. DUKE OUR WARMEST WELCOME TO THE REDSKINS ORGANIZATION!"..OKAY, WE'LL TAKE QUESTIONS NOW..

MR. DUKE, AS FAR AS WE CAN TELL, YOU BRING NO RELEVANT EXPERIENCE TO YOUR JOB. COULD YOU COMMENT?

YEAH. THAT'S A COMPLETE BUNCH OF GARBAGE.

BESIDES MY RECORD IN ADMINISTRATION, I BRING TO MY JOB AN AWESOME EXPERTISE IN SPORTS MEDICINE. IT WILL BE MY DUTY TO SEE THAT EACH AND EVERY MAN IS SAFELY WIRED BEFORE HE GOES OUT ON THAT BALL FIELD!

WHAT? YOU MEAN YOU'LL ACTUALLY BE DISPENSING PILLS?

YES. MY CONTRACT EXPLICITLY..

THANKS FOR COMING, BOYS!

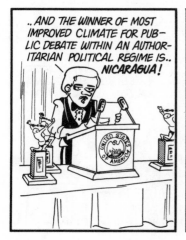

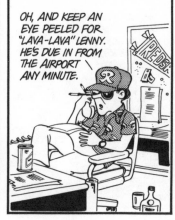

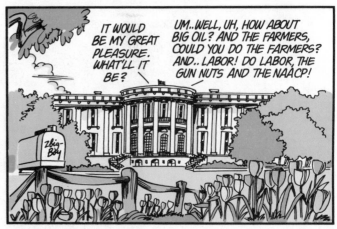

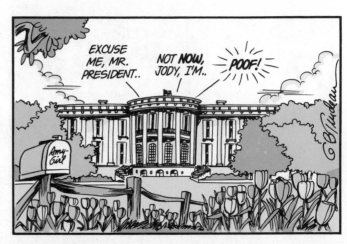

Panel 1: HI, THIS IS ABC! FREDDY SILVERMAN'S OFFICE! / HELLO, THIS IS IRWIN NUMBERS AT NBC. IS FRED IN?

Panel 2: I'M SORRY, SIR, MR. SILVERMAN'S ABC CONTRACT IS NOT UP UNTIL NEXT WEEK. HE IS NOT PERMITTED TO.. / TO TALK TO ME, YES, I KNOW. COULD YOU GIVE HIM A MESSAGE FOR ME, THEN? IT'S VERY IMPORTANT!

Panel 3: VERY WELL, SIR. / TELL HIM WE'RE ON THE VERGE OF ANNOUNCING THE NEW SHOW WE DISCUSSED, BUT THAT THERE'S REAL CONCERN THAT THE STAR ISN'T STACKED ENOUGH.

Panel 4: I'LL SEE THAT HE GETS THE MESSAGE, SIR. / TELL HIM IT'S URGENT, OKAY? WE'VE ALREADY GOT TWO SHOWS IN THE CAN.

Panel 5: WE'RE REALLY APPRECIATIVE YOU COULD COME OVER FOR A PEEK AT THE SHOW, FRED.. FREDDY!

Panel 6: THE NAME IS FREDDY! **NEVER** CALL ME FRED! WHEN'RE YOU PEOPLE GOING TO LEARN? TO PROGRAM FOR NINE-YEAR-OLDS, YOU HAVE TO **THINK** LIKE ONE!

Panel 7: IF YOU WANT NBC TO START CLICKING AGAIN, YOU'RE GOING TO HAVE TO **STOP** ACTING LIKE GROWN MEN! UNDERSTOOD? / YES, FREDDY.

Panel 8: GOOD. NOW, LET'S TAKE A LOOK AT YOUR CLEAVAGE SITUATION. / RIGHT. OKAY, IN THIS FIRST EPISODE, THE PLOT CALLED FOR WET T-SHIRTS..

Panel 9: LET ME SET IT UP FOR YOU, FREDDY. THE GUY ON THE LEFT IS LEONARD. HE RUNS A WOMEN'S HEALTH SPA IN LOS ANGELES!

Panel 10: OUR JIGGLE INTEREST IS MUFFY, THE PHYSICAL THERAPIST. THE RUNNING GAG IS THAT EVERY TIME LEONARD GOES IN TO CHECK THE SAUNA, THERE'S MUFFY!

Panel 11: WE THINK THAT CHRISSY LANG, THE GIRL WHO PLAYS MUFFY, IS A MAJOR, BUT MAJOR, TALENT! WE THINK SHE COULD MAKE "SPA" THE HOTTEST SHOW ON T.V.!

Panel 12: GREAT STUFF. DOES SHE HAVE ANY LINES? / WELL, NOT AT FIRST. WE WANT TO ESTABLISH HER CHARACTER.

Panel 13: ..AND THE VIEWER SOON SEES THAT LEONARD'S FAMILY IS A LOT LIKE HIS OWN, ONLY MUCH ZANIER! / DON'T TALK WITH YOUR MOUTH FULL, DEAR! / AW, MOM!

Panel 14: NOW, THIS NEXT BIT INTRODUCES SALLY, THE TEEN-AGED DAUGHTER. / HEY! LOOK WHO'S FINALLY UP!

Panel 15: 'MORNING, EVERYONE!

Panel 16: HEY! FULL FRONTAL NUDITY! I **LOVE** IT! / WELL, WAIT'LL YOU SEE THE PREDICAMENTS SHE GETS IN! / ANYONE SEEN MY SHAMPOO?

THIS IS ROLAND BURTON HEDLEY, JR.! AT ROCKEFELLER CENTER TONIGHT, TENSIONS ARE MOUNTING AS THE NBC TELEVISION NETWORK AWAITS ITS NEW MESSIAH, FRED P. SILVERMAN.

CAN THE GENIUS BEHIND "THE LOVE BOAT" AND "CAPTAIN CAVEMAN AND THE TEENANGELS" RESTORE THE FORTUNES OF LASTPLACE NBC? A RECENT DEVELOPMENT SUGGESTS HE MIGHT..

ABC WIDE WORLD OF NEWS HAS LEARNED THAT WHEN FREDDY SILVERMAN ARRIVES AT NBC THIS WEEK, HE WILL PROPOSE A POLICY OF PRIME-TIME FRONTAL NUDITY!

ALSO, CHIMPS. BUT WE'LL GET TO THAT LATER. FOR DETAILS ON THE NUDITY, LET'S GO TO CHICAGO..

CHICAGO?

YES, AS THE COUNTDOWN CONTINUES, THE NAME OF THE GAME AT NBC IS "WAITING FOR FREDDY."

CAN SILVERMAN TURN THINGS AROUND FOR THE LOWLY NETWORK? WELL, IT'S ANYONE'S GUESS. IN THE RATINGS GAME THERE IS ONLY ONE QUESTION: HOW LOW ARE YOU WILLING TO SINK?

NO ONE, IT SEEMS, IS IMMUNE. EVEN THE NEW TAG-TEAM ANCHOR FORMAT RIGHT HERE AT ABC WIDE WORLD OF NEWS WAS ADOPTED AS A DESPERATE, LAST-DITCH RESPONSE TO SAGGING RATINGS.

BACK TO YOU, FRANK, PETER, AND MAX. THANKS.

THANK YOU, ROLLIE.

YES, THANKS. IN OTHER NEWS..

THE LONG VIGIL IS OVER. EVEN AS I SPEAK, FRED P. SILVERMAN IS SPINNING HIS MILLION-DOLLAR WHEELS FOR THIRD-PLACE NBC!

ALREADY, THE NEW MAN HAS BEGUN TO LIVE UP TO HIS IMAGE AS A HARD WORKER. SILVERMAN IS SAID TO HAVE REPORTED TO WORK THIS MORNING AT 5:30 A.M.!

AND NOW, ADMIDST GROWING RUMORS THAT THEIR NEW BOSS EVEN SKIPPED LUNCH, NBC EXECUTIVES ARE ANXIOUSLY AWAITING THE OUTCOME OF FREDDY'S PROGRAMING MAGIC!

ANY CHANGE YET?

YES..YES! BY GOD, HE'S TURNING IT AROUND!

LOOK OUT, WONDER CHIMP!

BLAM! BLAM!

FRED SILVERMAN. ON TOP. THE MAN OF THE MOMENT. BUT WHAT OF THE LOSERS? WHAT HAPPENS TO THEM? CORRESPONDENT ROLAND HEDLEY TALKED TO THE SECRETARY OF NBC'S DEPOSED HERB SCHLOSSER.

MISS JENKINS, WHAT WAS IT LIKE TO WORK FOR HERB SCHLOSSER?

WHO? I DON'T RECALL ANYONE BY THAT NAME.

COME NOW, MISS JENKINS, FOR THE LAST TWELVE YEARS YOU WERE HIS PER..

I DON'T KNOW HIM, I TELL YOU! LEAVE ME ALONE!

FOR MORE ON THE STORY, WE HAVE THIS REPORT FROM SIBERIA.

SPRING COMES LATE TO THE URAL MOUNTAINS..

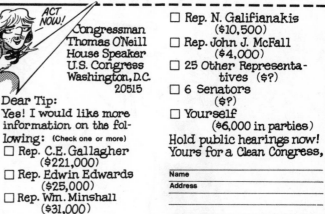

THE FALL OF MALIBU

Q: Tell us about Zonker's beach.

A: Well, technically, it's not really his beach. It's simply named after him. The Zonker Harris Memorial Beach. It was one of the private Malibu beaches recently liberated by the California Coastal Commission.[1] The residents were, of course, furious, and the redwood sign marking the access route was vandalized within twenty-four hours.

[1]Don Neuwirth, the project manager, told the *Los Angeles Times* that beach access in Malibu was a victory for the public. "If you take a picture of us erecting the sign," he said, "try to make it look like the raising of the flag at Iwo Jima."

CALIFORNIA STATE TANNING BUREAU, MAY I HELP YOU?

YEAH, COULD YOU TELL ME IF YOUR TANNING CLINICS WILL BE OPENING THIS SUMMER?

I'M AFRAID WE DON'T KNOW YET, SIR. WE HAVEN'T RECEIVED THE NEW BUDGET. I'D BE HAPPY TO TAKE YOUR RESERVATION, THOUGH.

UM..OKAY. GOT ANY ROOM LEFT AT YOUR MALIBU FACILITY?

SORRY, SIR, MALIBU IS BOOKED SOLID FOR THE SUMMER.

BIG SUR, THEN?

WAITING LIST. HOW ABOUT OAKLAND?

WELL, ALL RIGHT, BUT I WANT A PRIVATE SUN DECK.

HI, POP!

SON! WHAT ARE YOU DOING HOME?

TANNING CLINIC! I START TODAY!

YOU MEAN YOU HAVEN'T HEARD? GOVERNOR BROWN JUST CLOSED THEM FOR THE SEASON. BECAUSE OF PROP 13.

WHAT?

THAT'S NOT ALL. HE'S ALSO CUT OUT THE SMALL CAR LOAN PROGRAM FOR MINORITY MOTORISTS.

IN CALIFORNIA? IS HE CRAZY?

I KNOW, I KNOW. IT'S ALWAYS THE PALE AND THE POOR WHO SUFFER FIRST.

THE TANNING CLINICS? DAD, I CAN'T GET OVER IT! HOW COULD BROWN CLOSE THE TANNING CLINICS?

WELL, SON, I SUSPECT WITH THE HIGH INCIDENCE OF SKIN CANCER IN THIS COUNTRY, IT WAS PROBABLY A POLITICALLY POPULAR THING TO DO.

BUT THAT'S SO SHORTSIGHTED! THE SUN IS ALSO THE GREAT PROGENITOR, THE SOURCE OF LIFE, OF LIGHT, OF MAGNIFICENT TANS!

TRUE, BUT THE GOVERNOR HAD A MANDATE FROM THE PEOPLE, SON.

I HATE THIS GODLESS CULTURE.

ME, TOO. EXCEPT FOR MARY TYLER MOORE.

YOU'RE TAKING THIS AWFUL HARD, SON..

I KNOW. IT'S JUST THAT IT'S SO UNFAIR..

I TRAINED SO HARD ALL WINTER WITH MY LAMP, HOPING, PRAYING, THAT I'D RAISE A DEEP ENOUGH TAN TO GET ME ACCEPTED AT A GOOD CLINIC! AND NOW.. THIS!

GEE, I'M SORRY, SON, I REALLY AM.

=SIGH=..

IS THERE ANYTHING I CAN DO?

NO..NO.. I JUST WANT TO BE ALONE WITH THE SUN FOR A WHILE, OKAY?

..AND.. LET'S SEE.. $200 ON THE RAMS WITH A 6-POINT SPREAD..

LORD, I LOVE THIS SPORT!

MAC, I CAN'T TELL YOU HOW GREAT IT IS YOU CAME ALL THIS WAY! "LAVA-LAVA" WILL BE THRILLED!

WELL, HE'S BECOME THE DARLING OF PAGO PAGO, GOVERNOR. THE LOCAL KIDS TALK OF NO ONE ELSE!

HE'S A PHENOMENON, MACARTHUR, THERE'S NO DOUBT ABOUT IT!

YOU'RE NOT DOING SO BAD YOURSELF, SIR. YOU SOUND BETTER THAN YOU HAVE IN YEARS!

WELL, IT'S THE COUNTRY, MAC. SINCE WE LAST LOCKED HORNS, IT'S GONE THROUGH A LOT OF CHANGES, CHANGES I NEVER THOUGHT POSSIBLE.

THE AMERICAN DREAM IS OVER, MAC. IT'S BEEN SHATTERED INTO A MILLION JAGGED PIECES. ALL THAT'S LEFT IS A NATION OF MIDDLE-CLASS HUSTLERS.

OUR INSTITUTIONS ARE IN RUINS, AND PUBLIC LIFE HAS BEEN RE-DUCED TO A DARWINIAN NIGHTMARE OF COMPETING SPECIAL INTERESTS. AS A PEOPLE, WE'VE BEEN STRIPPED OF THE LAST VES-TIGES OF MORAL PURPOSE!

IT MUST BE AN EXCITING TIME FOR YOU, SIR.

WELL, I MEAN, TALK ABOUT THE GROUND FLOOR.

LIKE BUYING POLAROID AT 4½, SIR.

G.B.Trudeau

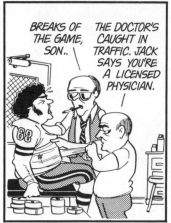

SO HOW'S EDDIE DOING, KID?

HE'S OUT FOR THE SEASON. AS ARE BOTH OF THE GUYS HE CLOTHESLINED.

SIR, I MAY BE A LITTLE OLD-FASHIONED, BUT ALL THESE OVER-AMPED PLAYERS BASHING EACH OTHER'S BRAINS OUT.. CAN THAT BE GOOD FOR THE GAME?

IT'S THE OWNERS, SON. THEY'RE BLIND TO THE PROBLEM. WITHOUT URINE TESTS, WHAT CAN I DO?

I DON'T KNOW, SIR, BUT RIGHT NOW YOU'RE PUTTING A LOT OF GUYS IN THE HOS-/PITAL!

HEY, LOOK, CHOIR BOY..

SIR, I'VE DECIDED TO GO TO THE PAPERS.

GO TO THE PAPERS? ARE YOU MAD, KID? YOU WANT TO GET THE WHOLE FRONT OFFICE BUSTED?

WELL, NO, SIR, BUT I JUST CAN'T SIT BY AND WATCH THE GAME RUINED BY HOMICIDAL SPEED-FREAKS!

LOOK, RILEY! THIS IS FOOTBALL! TO QUOTE HARRY TRUMAN, IF YOU CAN'T TAKE THE HEAT, THEN GET THE HELL OUT OF NAGASAKI!

YOU LETTING ME GO, SIR?

WELL, NOW THAT YOU MENTION IT, THAT'S A DAMN GOOD..

"BOY, 15, AXED BY REDSKINS' DRUG DOC."

SIT DOWN, RILEY..

IT'S TOO LATE FOR THAT, SIR.

HELLO?

HELLO, IS THIS RICK REDFERN, ACE INVESTIGATIVE REPORTER FOR THE "POST"?

NOT ACCORDING TO MY EDITOR.

I HAVE SOMETHING FOR YOU, SIR. LISTEN CAREFULLY..

THE INJURIES IN LAST SUNDAY'S REDSKINS GAME? THEY WEREN'T JUST BAD LUCK. THE PLAYER RESPONSIBLE WAS STONED OUT OF HIS GOURD AT THE TIME! INTERESTED?

NOT REALLY. HOW OLD ARE YOU, SON?

I'LL BE IN TOUCH. >CLICK!=

..AND IF YOU WANT TO HEAR THE WHOLE TAWDRY STORY, MEET ME AT ZEIBERT'S AT 12:30 SHARP!

12:30 AT ZEIBERT'S. GOT IT.

I MUST HAVE YOUR WORD, THOUGH, MR. REDFERN. MY IDENTITY MUST BE PROTECTED. I HAVE TOO MUCH TO LOSE.

WELL, OKAY, FELLAH. BUT I DON'T KNOW HOW MUCH OF A STORY THAT WILL LEAVE ME.

DON'T WORRY, THIS STORY WILL WRITE ITSELF.

IT WILL?

"INFORMED SOURCE, 15, ROCKS NFL."

NOT BAD.. HOW WILL I KNOW YOU?

YOUR FOOTBALL ARTICLE SEEMS TO BE CAUSING QUITE A STIR, RICHARD..

YEAH, THAT GUY DUKE SURE DOESN'T TAKE THINGS LYING DOWN.

HE RELEASED A 2,000 WORD REBUTTAL YESTERDAY, AND TODAY HE'S HOLDING A PRESS CONFERENCE IN HIS OFFICE..

HE CLAIMS HE'S EVEN GOING TO PRODUCE THE INJURED PLAYER TO TESTIFY ON HIS BEHALF!

I DUNNO, SIR, HE DOESN'T LOOK SO GOOD..

NURSE! CUT THIS MAN DOWN!

..AND DESPITE MY HEATED PROTESTATIONS, EDDIE HAS CRAWLED FROM HIS HOSPITAL BED TO JOIN ME IN OUTRAGED DENIAL OF THIS ALLEGED PIECE OF REPORTING!

THIS ARTICLE REPRESENTS THE SHODDIEST KIND OF JOURNALISM! NAMES, DATES, PLACES ARE ALL INACCURATE! EVEN DOSAGES ARE DISTORTED AND TAKEN TOTALLY OUT OF CONTEXT!

AS EDDIE VIGOROUSLY CONFIRMS, THE "CONTROLLED SUBSTANCES" I GAVE HIM IN LAST SUNDAY'S GAME WERE NOTHING MORE THAN COMMON ASPIRIN TABLETS! RIGHT, EDDIE?

MMPHH.

NOW, I HOPE WE'VE HEARD THE LAST OF THIS SILLY EPISODE!

>WHEEZE!< COUGH! COUGH!

WHILE WE'RE ALL HERE, I'D LIKE TO TAKE THE OPPORTUNITY TO COMMENT FURTHER ON REDFERN'S INFLAMMATORY PROSE..

UNNHH..

IT IS A SORRY STATE OF AFFAIRS WHEN A POLITICAL REPORTER IS SENT TO COVER FOOTBALL, A SUBJECT HE IS CLEARLY UNEQUIPPED TO COMMENT ON!

UNNH.. ARRGH!

OBVIOUSLY, IN FOOTBALL PEOPLE GET HURT! BUT IT IS THE RISK OF INJURY THAT MAKES THE GAME GREAT! IT IS THE COURAGE OF ATHLETES AS THEY..

BONK!

EDDIE, WILL YOU SETTLE DOWN? THIS IS IMPORTANT.

>CHIRP!< CAW! CAW!

>RIBBIT! RIBBIT!<

GOOD EVENING. I'M ROLAND BURTON HEDLEY, JR., AND THAT WAS THE SCENE TODAY AT CAMP DAVID, SITE OF JIMMY CARTER'S DAZZLING MIDEAST SUMMITRY!

WHAT REALLY WENT ON DURING THOSE THIRTEEN DAYS IN SEPTEMBER? JOIN US AS ABC WIDE WORLD OF NEWS TAKES AN IN-DEPTH LOOK AT..CABIN FEVER!

"CABIN FEVER: FOOTPATHS TO GLORY," BROUGHT TO YOU BY..

>CHIRP!<

>TWITTER!<

CABIN FEVER
abc Wide World Special Report

CABIN FEVER. FOR THIRTEEN LONG DAYS, IT HELD THE WORLD IN ITS GRIP.

WHAT WENT ON IN THOSE SMALL BUT ATTRACTIVELY APPOINTED COTTAGES AT CAMP DAVID? ABC WIDE WORLD OF NEWS RE-CREATES THE ACTION!

DAY ONE. IT'S A LAZY, WARM AFTERNOON AS PRESIDENT ANWAR SADAT'S HELICOPTER TOUCHES DOWN AT CAMP DAVID..

ROLLIE?

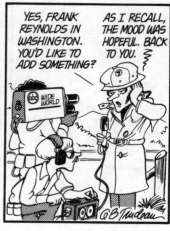

YES, FRANK REYNOLDS IN WASHINGTON. YOU'D LIKE TO ADD SOMETHING?

AS I RECALL, THE MOOD WAS HOPEFUL. BACK TO YOU.

DAY FIVE. THE ISRAELIS CLIMB TO NEW HEIGHTS OF INFLEXIBILITY. BEGIN'S INTRANSIGENCE HANGS OVER THE CAMP LIKE A WET BLANKET.

STILL, OCCASIONAL LEVITY CUTS THROUGH THE GLOOM. DURING AN EARLY MORNING STROLL, BEGIN REMARKS TO CARTER, "THIS PLACE IS LIKE HEAVEN ON EARTH."

THE PRESIDENT, SENSING AN OPENING, OFFERS HIM CAMP DAVID. BEGIN, SENSING A RETIREMENT HOME, ACCEPTS.

IF ONLY FOR A MOMENT, CAMP DAVID RINGS WITH LAUGHTER.

DAY TEN. THE MARCH TOWARD PEACE FLOUNDERS. AS TEMPERS FLARE AND ANTES ARE UPPED, JIMMY CARTER ACTS. A TOP AMERICAN NEGOTIATOR REMEMBERS.

WELL, HE SCHEDULED A MOVIE, "PATTON." IT WAS A RATHER COURAGEOUS ACT OF PROGRAMING, SINCE THE SAME FILM ONCE INSPIRED NIXON TO INVADE CAMBODIA.

THE EFFECT WAS QUITE DIFFERENT ON THE ISRAELIS, THOUGH. AFTER ONE ESPECIALLY GORY SCENE, DEFENSE MINISTER WEIZMAN ROSE AND CRIED OUT, "NEVER AGAIN!" THE IMPASSE WAS BROKEN.

COMING UP: PEACE ON THE RAMPAGE.

AMERICAN NEGOTIATOR, IN YOUR OWN WORDS, DESCRIBE THE MOOD AS DAY THIRTEEN BROKE AT CAMP DAVID. IT WAS ONE OF UNCERTAINTY, WAS IT NOT?

THAT'S RIGHT, ROLAND. EVEN AFTER THE CLIMACTIC SADAT-CARTER MEETING IN ASPEN LODGE, THE SUCCESS OF THE SUMMIT WAS STILL IN DOUBT..

AS SADAT WAS LEAVING HIS CABIN, HE BUMPED INTO THE ISRAELI PRIME MINISTER. OFFERING HIS HAND, HE SMILED AND SAID, "LET US BEGIN, BEGIN."

AND BEGIN REPLIED?

"WE'RE NOT OUT OF THE WOODS YET."

STILL DOTTING THE "i"s, EH?

..AND WITH THE RESTORATION OF THE SINAI CAME THE RETURN OF VITAL OIL FIELDS. IN ECONOMIC TERMS, IT WAS A SIGNIFICANT CONCESSION!

REMEMBER, LANGUAGE WAS REALLY THE KEY TO THE NEGOTIATIONS. EACH SIDE HAD ITS OWN TERMINOLOGY FOR DESCRIBING A GIVEN GEO-POLITICAL SITUATION.

FOR INSTANCE, MR. SADAT KEPT REFERRING TO THE WEST BANK AS AN "INADMISSIBLY OCCUPIED TERRITORY."

AND MR. BEGIN?

BEGIN CALLED IT "THE LAND OF MILK AND HONEY."

DAIRY PRODUCTS? THAT'S A NEW TWIST, ISN'T IT?

TOP AMERICAN NEGOTIATOR, IT WASN'T ALL PEACHES AND CREAM AT CAMP DAVID, WAS IT? IN FACT, YOU HAD YOUR SHARE OF LOW WATER MARKS, RIGHT?

THAT'S RIGHT, ROLAND, I'D SAY THE WORST MOMENT CAME WHEN BEGIN ACCUSED SADAT OF DELIBERATELY ATTACKING WHILE ISRAELIS WORSHIPED FOR YOM KIPPUR IN 1973.

HOW DID SADAT RESPOND?

AT FIRST, WITH SOME DIFFICULTY.

AND THEN?

THEN HE ACCUSED BEGIN OF TRYING TO LAY A GUILT TRIP ON HIM.

DOES SEEM LIKE A BIT OF A CHEAP SHOT..

DAY 15: CAMP DAVID PLUS TWO. THE HISTORIC PEACE ACCORDS KINDLE AN OUTPOURING OF PUBLIC ACCLAIM!

FOR CARTER, SUCCESS IS SWEET. HIS STANDING WITH CONGRESS AND WITH THE AMERICAN PEOPLE HAS NEVER BEEN ON FIRMER GROUND.

CASE IN POINT: IN THE WAKE OF CAMP DAVID, A NEW POLL REVEALS THAT 93% OF THE PUBLIC NOW FEELS THAT PRESIDENT CARTER IS DOING AN EXCELLENT JOB FIGHTING INFLATION.

MOREOVER, 86% NOW APPROVE OF HIS HANDLING OF THE LANCE AFFAIR..

WELL, I ALWAYS HAVE.

ME, TOO. HE'S BEEN JUST GREAT!

DAY 16. BEFORE MR. BEGIN DEPARTS FOR HOME, HE GRANTS AN EXCLUSIVE INTERVIEW TO ABC NEWS. HE IS ASKED IF HE HAS ANY PLANS FOR TAKING A VACATION..

ABSOLUTELY NOT! AS I TOLD NBC YESTERDAY, THE STRUGGLE FOR US NEVER ENDS. THE JEWISH PEOPLE MUST NEVER LET DOWN THEIR GUARD AGAINST THE ENEMY!

WE HAVE SUFFERED FOR TOO LONG, WE HAVE ENDURED PERSECUTION, HORRIBLE WARS, AND THE THREAT OF EXTINCTION FOR OVER TWO THOUSAND YEARS, BEGINNING WITH..

ABC NEWS WITHDREW THE QUESTION. BACK AFTER THIS..

WHAT DO THE NEW ACCORDS SPELL FOR MR. BEGIN'S CAREER? IN A FAR-RANGING INTERVIEW, I ASKED THE DOUR LITTLE EX-TERRORIST ABOUT HIS POLITICAL FUTURE..

WELL, AS I TOLD CBS EARLIER, MR. HEDLEY, SOME FRIENDS WILL CRITICIZE ME. BUT THAT IS THEIR RIGHT. IT IS TO BE EXPECTED. THERE IS A PHILOSOPHICAL EXPRESSION FOR THIS..

SWITCHING FROM ENGLISH, MR. BEGIN THEN SPOKE DIRECTLY TO HIS OWN PEOPLE..

.."C'EST LA VIE."

CABIN FEVER PLUS TWO WEEKS. THE DRAMA COMES TO A CLOSE..

THE TWO WEEKS OF DAY-AND-NIGHT SUMMITRY FINALLY CATCH UP WITH AN EXHAUSTED PRESIDENT..

TAKING THE EVENING OFF, MR. CARTER HEADS OUT TO RFK STADIUM, WHERE HE IS THE HONORED GUEST OF THE MANAGEMENT OF THE WASHINGTON REDSKINS FOOTBALL CLUB..

JUST COFFEE. WHY?

FOR THIRTEEN STRAIGHT DAYS? C'MON, SIR, YOU CAN TELL ME!

HEY, KIRBY! WHY THE LONG FACE?

I'M AT ODDS WITH MY ERA, ZONKER.

OF COURSE, YOU ARE, KIRBY. WHAT ARE YOU TALKING ABOUT?

GROWING UP IN THE SEVENTIES. I CAN'T SEEM TO ATTACH ANY MEANING TO IT..

HERE WE ARE, ALMOST NINE YEARS INTO THE DECADE, AND THE MAJOR CULTURAL CONTRIBUTION OF THE SEVENTIES IS A FIFTIES REVIVAL CRAZE!

OH, C'MON, KIRBY! WHAT ABOUT DISCO? AND WATERGATE BOOKS?

WELL, OKAY, BUT HOW MANY OTHER BRIGHT SPOTS WERE THERE?

I DON'T QUITE UNDERSTAND, KIRBY. WHAT EXACTLY IS WRONG WITH THE SEVENTIES?

THEY LACK DEFINITION, Z. I DON'T FEEL LIKE I LIVE IN AN ERA I CAN REALLY CALL MY OWN!

OH, I'VE SHOPPED AROUND, OF COURSE. I'VE CHECKED OUT ALL THE TOP-GROSSING PERIOD FILMS, "GREASE," "ANIMAL HOUSE," "COMING HOME," ETC., BUT NONE OF THEM IS REALLY ME. I GUESS YOU COULD SAY I'M A PEG IN SEARCH OF A HOLE!

ROUND OR SQUARE?

DOESN'T MATTER. AS LONG AS IT CAN SUPPORT THE WEIGHT OF MY CONVICTIONS.

BOY, YOU REALLY ARE DEPRESSED..

DO YOU REALIZE I HAVE ABSOLUTELY NO MEMORY OF THE FORD YEARS?

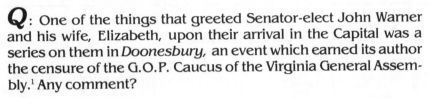
Q: One of the things that greeted Senator-elect John Warner and his wife, Elizabeth, upon their arrival in the Capital was a series on them in *Doonesbury,* an event which earned its author the censure of the G.O.P. Caucus of the Virginia General Assembly.[1] Any comment?

A: Sure. Better late than never. I had always assumed that the State of Virginia would spare itself the embarrassment of sending the Warners to Washington, but I'm as hopeless a handicapper as I am an optimist. Having missed the boat, I settled for a recap of some of the highlights of the campaign.[2] From the beginning, Warner's deployment of his assets, which is to say his wife and his money, was an absolute marvel, although losing the primary, as he somehow managed to do, was one of those things which gives opportunism a bad name. Fortunately, Providence interceded. His opponent was killed in an airplane crash, and John redeemed himself by immediately volunteering to replace him. Talk about your early bird...

[1]According to the AP, the motion's sponsor, State Senator Wiley Mitchell, announced, "I don't think we should sit placidly by and let the gnomes of the world run over us without expressing indignation."

[2]Warner later told the *Washington Post,* "The facts in the strip are totally false and inaccurate. Oh, I'm not going to pick them out. The people of Virginia know the facts."

You are cordially invited to a Media Event in honor of Senator and Mrs. Elizabeth Taylor

THIS ISN'T HAPPENING.. SIR! IT'S ME, HONEY!

I DON'T GET IT. I'M A RESPONSIBLE CONSUMER.. (THIS IS MR. DUKE. I USED TO BE HIS TRANSLATOR!)

I ONLY USE THE BEST PRODUCT. I NEVER MISCALCULATE DOSAGES.. I'M AN EXCHANGE STUDENT NOW! RIGHT HERE AT GEORGETOWN!

SO WHY AM I SURROUNDED BY TINY, PANTING ORIENTALS? (HE'S REALLY A GREAT GUY. HE'S JUST A LITTLE SHY.)

WELL! THE STUDENTS CERTAINLY SEEM TO BE FASCINATED BY YOUR MR. DUKE!

UH-HUH. SAY, WHO'S THE YOUNG LADY WHO HAS BEEN MONOPOLIZING HIM? THAT'S MS. HUAN. SHE'S FROM PEKING.

ACCORDING TO HER, SHE AND MR. DUKE WERE CLOSE FRIENDS DURING HIS TOUR OF DUTY IN CHINA..

WILL YOU BE SHOWING ME WASHINGTON BY NIGHT, SIR? CAN'T MAKE ANY SUDDEN MOVES.. HAVE TO STAY CALM..

EXCUSE ME, SIRS. I WONDER IF YOU COULD TELL ME WHERE I MIGHT FIND MR. DUKE.. SHOULD BE IN THE CLUBHOUSE, MISS. FIRST DOOR ON THE RIGHT.

THANK YOU. NOT AT ALL.

MAY I JUST SAY YOU'RE QUITE A PAIR OF SPECIMENS, SIRS. PART OF THE JOB, MISS. YOU SHOULD SEE THE GUYS WHO START.

THERE YOU ARE, SIR! OH, NO..

I'VE BEEN LOOKING ALL OVER FOR YOU! I'VE JUST BEEN TALKING TO YOUR RESERVE QUARTERBACK! WHAT A GREAT GUY! THIS BETTER BE AN AFTEREFFECT..

LISTEN, I THINK YOU SHOULD PLAY HIM. HE'S MUCH BETTER LOOKING THAN THE GUY YOU GOT PLAYING NOW. USED TO BE A TIME WHEN YOU KNEW WHAT WENT INTO THIS STUFF..

UM.. YOU'RE NOT GOING TO CHANGE FOR OUR DATE, SIR? THAT DOES IT! I'M SWITCHING PHARMACISTS!

I'M CERTAINLY LOOKING FORWARD TO OUR DATE TONIGHT, SIR. THE OTHER GIRLS IN MY DORM SAY THE NIGHT LIFE HERE IS REALLY SOMETHING!

YOU'RE NOT GOING TO TAKE ME TO A DISCO, ARE YOU, SIR? I MEAN, I'M NOT SURE IF THAT'S ALLOWED. I'D HAVE TO CHECK WITH THE EMBASSY FIRST.

IT'S REALLY YOU, ISN'T IT?

YES, SIR. I CHANGED MY HAIR A LITTLE. THAT MAY BE THROWING YOU.

YOU KNOW, SIR, IT WAS MORE THAN JUST A HAPPY ACCIDENT, US BUMPING INTO EACH OTHER LIKE WE DID..

IN FACT, THE FIRST THING I DID AFTER CLEARING CUSTOMS WAS CALL THE STATE DEPARTMENT TO FIND OUT WHERE YOU WERE!

IMAGINE MY SURPRISE WHEN I LEARNED YOU WERE RIGHT HERE IN WASHINGTON, WORKING WITH THE NATIVE AMERICANS!

REDSKINS.

RIGHT. IT'S SO LIKE YOU TO BE HELPING OUT OTHERS, SIR.

I'M SORRY, HONEY, I JUST HAVEN'T THE TIME TO DEAL WITH YOU RIGHT NOW..

WHERE YOU GOING, SIR?

ZEIBERT'S. I'M GOING TO HAVE A FEW BEERS, AND THEN WATCH THE DALLAS GAME. BY MYSELF!

WHAT IS ZEIBERT'S, SIR? SOME SORT OF "JOINT"?

THIS IS BUSINESS, HONEY. I'M AFRAID I CAN'T ASK YOU TO..

DON'T TELL ME YOU'RE GOING TO SHOW ME THE SOFT UNDERBELLY OF WASHINGTON NIGHTCLUB LIFE?

THE WHAT?

DON'T YOU THINK WE BETTER MAKE RESERVATIONS?

SIR, I PROPOSE THAT WE TOAST THE UNLIKELY BUT FELICITOUS SEQUENCE OF EVENTS THAT HAS BROUGHT US TOGETHER AGAIN!

EAST AND WEST REUNITED! OUTSTRETCHED HANDS, TREMBLING WITH EXCITEMENT, CLASPED IN PEACE! SHALL WE DRINK TO THAT, SIR?

SIR?

HONEY, YOU BETTER DITCH THAT MAO JACKET BEFORE SOMEONE TAKES A SHOT AT YOU.

OH, NO, SIR, IT GETS ME ALL SORTS OF DISCOUNTS.

ANYTHING FOR ME FROM THE AUDUBON SOCIETY, DEAREST?

NO..NO, IT LOOKS LIKE NOTHING BUT BILLS.

BILLS? THEY CERTAINLY DON'T WASTE ANY TIME ONCE CHRISTMAS IS OVER, DO THEY?

NO, THEY DON'T..OH, HERE'S AN INVITATION!

"YOU ARE CORDIALLY INVITED TO A SMALL MEDIA EVENT HONORING SENATOR AND MRS. ELIZABETH TAYLOR.."

TO WHAT?

WHO?

HOW EXCITING! WE'VE BEEN ASKED TO THE OPENING SALVO!

BUT, DEAREST! IT'S THE VERY FIRST PARTY FOR ELIZABETH TAYLOR AND HER CONSORT!

I'M SORRY, LACEY, YOU'LL JUST HAVE TO GO BY YOURSELF..

I'VE GOT BETTER THINGS TO DO THAN GO ALL THE WAY ACROSS TOWN JUST TO MEET THE WIFE OF SOME DIM DILETTANTE WHO MANAGED TO BUY, MARRY AND LUCK HIS WAY INTO THE U.S. SENATE!

BUT, SWEETEST! I HAVE TO GO! THEY'RE REPUBLICANS!

WELL, I DON'T SEE HOW THAT'S OUR FAULT. THAT'S THE TROUBLE WITH THE G.O.P.—ANYBODY CAN JOIN!

OH, C'MON, DICK, JUST THIS ONCE. THEN WE'LL IGNORE THEM!

WELL, IF YOU MUST. BUT I'M WAITING IN THE CAR.

NOW, STOP CARRYING ON, DICK! I'M SURE JOHN WARNER GOT TO THE SENATE ON HIS OWN MERITS!

OH, C'MON, LACEY. REMEMBER WHEN THE PARTY'S ORIGINAL NOMINEE DIED IN THAT ACCIDENT?

THE WARNERS WERE SO STRICKEN WITH SYMPATHY THAT THEY OFFERED TO TAKE ON THE CAMPAIGN DEBT AND TO SET UP A TRUST FUND FOR THE FAMILY. GUESS WHO WAS THEN TAPPED THE NEXT DAY?

WELL, THEY DIDN'T HAVE TO OFFER ANYTHING, DICK..

CAN'T YOU JUST HEAR HIM MAKING HIS CASE? "I'LL SHOW YOU MY QUID IF YOU SHOW ME YOUR QUO!"

NOW, DICK, YOU'VE BEEN AROUND POLITICS LONG ENOUGH TO..

TO GROW CYNICAL? NEVER! I'M CONSTANTLY AMAZED!

LACEY! DEAREST! I'VE BEEN LOOKING ALL OVER FOR YOU!

WE JUST ARRIVED, GAIL. SORRY WE'RE SO LATE!

DON'T BE SILLY! I WAS JUST AFRAID YOU WEREN'T COMING..

WELL, AS YOU KNOW, DEAR, I'M NOT WILD ABOUT FILM PEOPLE. BUT LIZ TAYLOR, WELL..

THRILLING, ISN'T IT? WAIT UNTIL YOU SEE HER! SHE'S..

WE KNOW. "A TAD OVERWEIGHT, BUT WITH VIOLET EYES TO DIE FOR."

WHY, DICK! I THOUGHT YOU JUST GOT HERE!

WE DID. THAT'S FROM ONE OF THEIR BUMPER STICKERS.

MR. DUKE? IT'S RILEY HERE..

RILEY! WHERE ARE YOU, BOY?

DOWNSTAIRS. THE BELLBOY SAID YOU WERE FINALLY UP, SO I..

RILEY, WHAT THE HELL AM I DOING IN MIAMI? WHAT'S GOING ON? I CAN'T REMEMBER A DAMN THING!

WELL, SIR, THERE WAS AN INCIDENT IN YOUR OFFICE AT REDSKIN PARK. A U.S. MARSHAL WAS INVOLVED..

YOU MEAN, I'M.. I'M..

YES, SIR. YOU'RE ON THE LAM.

DAMN! I KNEW IT! GET UP HERE AND GIVE ME A HAND WITH THESE MATTRESSES!

FOR GOD'S SAKE, SIT DOWN, BOY! BEFORE SOMEONE RECOGNIZES US!

OH, DON'T WORRY, SIR. NO ONE COULD POSSIBLY KNOW YOU'RE IN TOWN..

DON'T BE SO SURE. WHAT DID I DO, ANYWAY?

WELL, SIR, IT ALL STARTED WHEN MR. WILLIAMS FIRED YOU LAST FRIDAY. YOU WOULDN'T LEAVE, SO HE GOT A COURT ORDER TO HAVE YOU REMOVED..

YOUR UNCLE SENT THE DAMN FEDS AFTER ME?

YES, SIR. BUT AS USUAL, WHEN THE MARSHALS TURNED UP, YOU ACTED LIKE YOU'D NEVER EVEN HEARD OF THE U.S. CRIMINAL CODE!

GOOD FOR ME! DAMN THING SHOULDA BEEN SCRAPPED YEARS AGO WHEN...

FORTUNATELY, YOU'RE NOT MUCH OF A SHOT.

MY GOD! YOU MEAN, I GOT INTO A FIREFIGHT WITH THE HEAT?

WELL, NOT A FIREFIGHT EXACTLY. YOU JUST SHOT OUT ALL THE FRONT WINDOWS AND TOOK OFF..

THAT NIGHT YOU CALLED ME FROM THE AIRPORT IN A RAGE. YOU SAID YOU KNEW THAT WILLIAMS WAS GOING TO BE AT THE SUPER BOWL, AND THAT YOU WERE GOING TO "TRACK HIM DOWN AND GREASE HIM" FOR FIRING YOU.

BEING HIS NEPHEW, I FELT I HAD AN OBLIGATION TO FIND YOU AND NIP THIS SICK, VIOLENT NOTION IN THE BUD! DON'T YOU RECALL ANY OF THIS, SIR?

A PLAN.. I MUST HAVE HAD A PLAN.

THINK, SIR! WAS THERE A GUN? I'VE GOT TO TRY TO STOP YOU!

I REALLY CAME ALL THE WAY DOWN HERE JUST TO WASTE WILLIAMS?

SIR, GIVE IT UP! IT CAN ONLY COME TO MORE GRIEF!

GIVE IT UP? KID, IN MY WHOLE LIFE, I..

SIR, IF YOU JUST FORGET THIS STUPID VENDETTA AND GO BACK TO COLORADO, I THINK I CAN PERSUADE MY UNCLE TO DROP THE CHARGES..

I CAN'T DO THAT, SON, THE REDSKINS NEED..

THE REDSKINS NEED COMPETENT MANAGEMENT, NOT ANOTHER YEAR OF FIXING AND PILLS!

YOU UNGRATEFUL PUP! DO YOU HAVE ANY IDEA WHAT THE SPREAD WAS BEFORE I ARRIVED?

I'LL GIVE YOU THREE HOURS. THEN I'M CALLING IN S.W.A.T.!

MR. SECRETARY, THE PEOPLE'S REPUBLIC OF CHINA VEHEMENTLY PROTESTS VIETNAM'S BRUTAL ARMORED ASSAULT INTO THE SOVEREIGN STATE OF KAMPUCHEA!

HANOI'S VILE AND SAVAGE BLITZKRIEG IS AN AFFRONT TO ALL PEACE-LOVING PEOPLES OF THE WORLD, AND SHOULD BE CONDEMNED BY THIS COUNCIL AS THE DESPICABLE, CRIMINAL ACT THAT IT IS!

AMBASSADOR PHRED, HOW DOES VIETNAM RESPOND?

AMBASSADOR PHRED?

SORRY, MR. SECRETARY, I WASN'T PLUGGED IN. WHAT ARE THE CHARGES AGAIN?

MR. SECRETARY, THIS IS AN OUTRAGE! THE AMBASSADOR FROM CHINA HAS NO GROUNDS WHATSOEVER FOR HIS CHARGE OF VIETNAMESE IMPERIALISM!

THE HOSTILITIES IN CAMBODIA WERE THE RESULT OF A POPULAR UPRISING AGAINST A BRUTAL REGIME! VIETNAM PLAYED ONLY A MINOR ADVISORY ROLE!

ADVISORY, MR. AMBASSADOR? THEN PERHAPS YOU COULD EXPLAIN TO THIS COUNCIL THE 100,000 SOLDIERS THAT POURED ACROSS THE BORDER ON DECEMBER 24!

WELL?

LOOK, THEY HEARD SHOTS. THEY WERE CURIOUS.

PHRED, YOUR DEFENSE TODAY OF VIETNAM'S ACTIONS WAS BRILLIANT, JUST BRILLIANT! I KNEW WHEN WE SIGNED THAT FRIENDSHIP ACCORD LAST YEAR YOU'D MAKE US PROUD!

WHY, THANK YOU, MR. AMBASSADOR.

YOU PEOPLE ARE DOING A GREAT JOB FOR US, JUST GREAT! KEEP IT UP!

WHO'S THAT, PHRED?

VIKTOR LOZINSKY, ONE OF OUR SOVIET FRIENDS.

SEEMS NICE.

ACTUALLY, HE'S A PIG, BUT THEY MAKE GREAT TANKS.

PHRED?

MIGUEL! WELCOME BACK! HOW'S EVERYTHING IN MANILA?

TO BE HONEST, PHRED, A BIT TENSE. SPEAKING FOR MY FELLOW DOMINOES, I SHOULD TELL YOU THAT YOUR COUNTRY'S LATEST REAL ESTATE GRAB HAS LEFT ALL OF US A LITTLE JUMPY.

OH, NOW, C'MON, MIGUEL—WITH CHINA CHAFING AT OUR BORDERS, YOU THINK WE NEED THE AGGRAVATION? BESIDES, OUR ASIAN NEIGHBORS ARE VALUED TRADING PARTNERS!

THEN I HAVE YOUR WORD?

WELL, NO, BUT I REALLY THINK YOU'RE BEING PARANOID.

GOOD EVENING. I'M ROLAND HEDLEY BURTON, JR. TONIGHT, ".30/.30" EXAMINES ONE OF THE STRANGEST PHENOMENA IN RECENT POLITICAL HISTORY..

HIS NAME IS EDWARD MOORE KENNEDY. HE IS THE SENIOR SENATOR FROM MASSACHUSETTS. BUT TO HIS THOUSANDS OF DEVOTED FOLLOWERS, HE IS KNOWN SIMPLY AS "TED."

WHO ARE THESE FOLLOWERS? WHERE DO THEY COME FROM? WHAT FORCE DRIVES THEM TO THROW GOOD MONEY AFTER BAD? TONIGHT, ABC WIDE WORLD OF NEWS LOOKS AT..

"THE LIBERAL CULT: THREAT FROM THE LEFT!"

The Liberal Cult
news abc close-up

THE LIBERAL CULT. HUMANE. JUST. FREE-SPENDING. AND UNDER THE GUIDANCE OF ITS CHARISMATIC LEADER, "TED". A MYSTERIOUS NEW FORCE ON THE POLITICAL SCENE!

WHO ARE THESE "LIBERALS"? HOW CAN WE ACCOUNT FOR THEIR CURIOUS APPEARANCE IN AN ERA OF FISCAL RESPONSIBILITY? WE ASKED CONSERVATIVE COLUMNIST DIRK DUPONT.

BEATS ME. I THOUGHT WE HAD THE SUCKERS UNDER CONTROL.

COMING UP: A LIBERAL'S MOTHER RECALLS HER SHAME.

WHAT SORT OF PERSON JOINS KENNEDY'S SO-CALLED "CULT OF CONSCIENCE"? WHAT EXACTLY IS A LIBERAL? ANTIOCH SOCIOLOGIST ALVIN RASHBAUM COMMENTS.

WELL, AS FAR AS WE CAN TELL, "TED" DRAWS HIS SUPPORTERS FROM THE RANKS OF PEOPLE WHO'VE NEVER HAD IT SO GOOD—BLACKS, WORKERS, THE ELDERLY, AND, OF COURSE, NEWLY ARRIVED BOAT PEOPLE.

THE TYPICAL LIBERAL FANTASIZES ABOUT BUILDING A JUST AND EGALITARIAN SOCIETY. WHAT HE DOESN'T UNDERSTAND, OF COURSE, IS THAT THESE THINGS COST MONEY.

IS HE DANGEROUS?

ONLY WHEN HE VOTES. HAPPILY, HE'S DISAFFECTED RIGHT NOW.

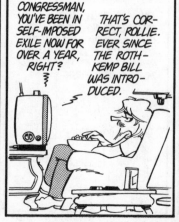
WHAT SORT OF SWAY DOES "TED" HAVE OVER HIS FOLLOWERS? I ASKED LIBERAL CONGRESSMAN BART SVIGALS, WHO FLED WASHINGTON DURING LAST YEAR'S OUTBREAK OF TAX-CUT FEVER..

CONGRESSMAN, YOU'VE BEEN IN SELF-IMPOSED EXILE NOW FOR OVER A YEAR, RIGHT?

THAT'S CORRECT, ROLLIE. EVER SINCE THE ROTH-KEMP BILL WAS INTRODUCED.

WOULD YOU RETURN TO CONGRESS IF SENATOR KENNEDY ASKED YOU TO?

YES, I WOULD. I WOULD DO ANYTHING FOR THE MAN.

WOULD YOU.. WOULD YOU OVERSPEND FOR HIM?

LAVISHLY. WITHOUT HESITATION.

I'LL BE PACKED IN A MINUTE, SPRINGFIELD. JUST MAKE YOURSELF COMFORTABLE.

QUITE A PLACE YOU HAVE HERE, MR. DUKE..

THANKS. I BUILT THIS CABIN MYSELF, BACK IN 1963. DID THE DECORATING AND EVERYTHING.

VERY NICE. MAY I ASK WHY YOU KEEP LAND MINES ON ALL THE SOFAS?

YEAH, I WAS TRYING TO TEACH THE DOGS TO STAY OFF THE FURNITURE.

WHAT DOGS?

OKAY, MR. DUKE, YOU'VE BEEN HERE BEFORE, SO I DON'T HAVE TO TELL YOU THAT THIS CONGRESS IS EVERY BIT AS SPINELESS AS ITS PREDECESSORS!

REMEMBER, THE LEGISLATORS WE DON'T OWN OUTRIGHT ARE SCARED TO DEATH OF MAIL! THEY'RE IN YOUR POCKET, MR. DUKE, SO WHEN YOU WALK THROUGH THAT DOOR, WALK TALL!

GOTCHA. I DON'T REALLY HAVE TO READ ALL OF THESE CRIME-STOPPER STORIES, DO I?

NO, NO, OF COURSE NOT. YOU JUST BE YOURSELF. YOU'RE OUR ACE IN THE HOLE, MR. DUKE!

I AM? WHAT HAPPENED TO THE WIDOW WHO WASTED NINE MUGGERS?

SHE FOLLOWS YOU. YOU'RE OUR NUMBER-ONE GUN!

"..AND IT IS THE POSITION OF THE NATIONAL RIFLE ASSOCIATION THAT WHEN IT COMES TO ARBITRARY SOCIAL CONTROLS, MORE IS LESS!"

"WHAT IS NEEDED INSTEAD IS A SENSE OF RESTRAINT AND FAIR PLAY. IF OUR ONCE PROUD SCHOOLS WERE TO RESUME THE TEACHING OF.."

EXCUSE ME, MR. DUKE..

I WANT TO GET THIS STRAIGHT. IS IT ACTUALLY YOUR VIEW THAT THE ANSWER TO RISING HANDGUN VIOLENCE IS A RENEWED EMPHASIS ON SPORTSMANSHIP?

YES?

EXACTLY. WE ADVOCATE A RETURN TO RESPONSIBLE GUNPLAY.

IN OUR ONCE PROUD—SCHOOLS?

"THE NATIONAL RIFLE ASSOCIATION THEREFORE OPPOSES ANY AND ALL LEGISLATIVE ATTEMPTS TO CONTROL OUR CONSTITUTIONAL RIGHT TO BEAR ARMS!"

THAT'S THE END OF OUR PREPARED STATEMENT, MR. CHAIRMAN. I'D BE HAPPY TO ENTERTAIN ANY QUESTIONS.

MR. DUKE, DOES YOUR GROUP'S OPPOSITION EXTEND TO A SIMPLE REQUIREMENT OF SERIAL NUMBERS TO AID POLICE IN IDENTIFICATION?

WHAT'S WRONG WITH DENTAL RECORDS?

I WAS REFERRING TO THE GUNS.

SENATOR, THE POINT IS THAT ONCE YOU HAVE GUN CONTROL, THE ONLY PEOPLE LEFT WITH GUNS ARE CRIMINALS!

WHICH WOULD PREVENT A *GREAT* MANY MURDERS, MR. DUKE!

AS YOU WELL KNOW, ALMOST 70% OF ALL MURDERS ARE COMMITTED AMONG FAMILY MEMBERS OR FRIENDS. AND OVER HALF OF THEM INVOLVE HAND-GUNS!

EXACTLY! SO LOOK AT IT FROM THE POINT OF VIEW OF THE VICTIM! WHAT IF *YOUR* WIFE WERE ATTACKING YOU WITH A HANDGUN?

I DON'T FOLLOW, MR. DUKE.

WELL, WOULDN'T YOU WANT TO BE IN A POSITION TO RETURN THE FIRE?

WELL, I..UH.. YOU DON'T HAVE TO ANSWER THAT, JIM.

THE QUESTION WE ARE FACING, THEN, MR. DUKE, IS WHETHER THE WISHES OF 80% OF THE AMERI-CAN PEOPLE WILL AGAIN GO UNHEEDED..

I CANNOT SPEAK FOR MY COLLEAGUES, BUT I FOR ONE AM *FED UP* WITH YOUR DEAD-LY LOBBY AND ITS FANATICAL DEFENSE OF A TRAGIC AND UNCONSCIONABLE PUBLIC POLICY!

I SEE.

SHALL I PUT YOU DOWN FOR A MILLION POST CARDS, THEN, SENATOR?

DON'T TRY TO INTIMI-DATE *ME*, MR. DUKE!

WE'RE BACK TALKING WITH DR. ALI MAHDAVI, '74, ON LEAVE FROM THE IRANIAN REVOLUTIONARY TRIBUNAL, AND HERE ON CAMPUS FOR HIS FIFTH REUNION!

DR. MAHDAVI, FOR OVER A YEAR NOW, AMERICANS HAVE BEEN HEARING ABOUT THE DARK, SINIS-TER SIDE OF IRAN'S BEARDED HOLY MAN.

I WONDER IF YOU COULD TELL US SOMETHING OF THE OTHER SIDE, THE HU-MAN SIDE..

SUCH AS?

WELL, LIKE WHAT DO BEARDED HOLY MEN HAVE FOR BREAKFAST?

SHAHS. IS THIS GOING TO TAKE LONG?

DR. MAHDAVI, HOW DO YOU RESPOND TO CRITICISM THAT YOUR NEW REVO-LUTIONARY GOVERNMENT IS RAPIDLY BECOMING THE WORSE OF TWO EVILS?

IT HAS BEEN CHARGED, FOR INSTANCE, THAT THE AYATOLLAH'S ISLAMIC REPUBLIC IS, IN EFFECT, RETURNING IRAN TO THE 14TH CENTURY!

WELL, YES, THAT WAS THE ORIGINAL PLAN, BUT IT IS ENTIRELY POSSIBLE THERE WILL BE SOME COMPROMISE ON THE EXACT ERA.

YOU MEAN, THERE'S A NEW TAR-GET DATE?

YES, SOME OF US ARE TRYING TO GET IT MOVED UP TO THE AGE OF VOLTAIRE.

AS YOU KNOW, DR. MAHDAVI, IN RECENT WEEKS, THERE HAS BEEN AN OUTPOURING OF PROTEST FROM IRANIAN WOMEN OVER THE ALL-COVERING "CHADOR," WHICH THEY SEE AS A SYMBOL OF ISLAMIC SEXISM.

WILL THE AYATOLLAH RESPOND TO THIS NEW..

IT HAS ALREADY BEEN RESOLVED. THE RULE ABOUT THE CHADOR WAS BEING TAKEN TOO LITERALLY.

THE AYATOLLAH DOES NOT DISAPPROVE OF OTHER FORMS OF DRESS, AS LONG AS THEY ARE MODEST. WHAT HE DOES OBJECT TO ARE SKIRTS AND GOWNS, THE GARMENTS OF PROSTITUTES!

I SEE. HOW ABOUT THE ANNIE HALL LOOK?

IF WORN WITH A VEIL, FINE.

DR. MAHDAVI, ABOUT HOW FAR CAN WE EXPECT THE NEW IRAN TO TAKE THE EXPULSION OF THE OLD WESTERN PRESENCE?

IT WILL BE COMPLETE. IT WILL BE TOTAL. THE IMMORALITY OF YOUR CULTURE HAS NO PLACE IN IRANIAN SOCIETY!

IT IS SOMETHING WE **CANNOT** COMPROMISE ON! WESTERN INFLUENCES AND CUSTOMS WILL SIMPLY NOT BE TOLERATED! OFFENDERS HAVE ALREADY BEEN PUT TO DEATH!

WHAT? YOU'VE **SEEN** THIS?

SEEN IT? I PERSONALLY CONDEMNED TWO JOGGERS.

DR. MAHDAVI, YOU AND MANY OTHER AMERICAN-EDUCATED IRANIANS HAVE COME A LONG WAY IN THE LAST YEAR — FROM GRADUATE SEMINAR ROOMS TO THE CORRIDORS OF POWER..

HOW DO YOU FEEL ABOUT YOUR REMARKABLE CHANGE OF FORTUNE?

OUR REVOLUTION HAS A SLOGAN WHICH SPEAKS TO THAT. IT IS THIS: "ALLAHU AKBAR!"!

WHICH MEANS?

IT MEANS, "GOD IS GREAT."

HOW TRUE! WE'LL BE BACK AFTER THIS!

OR, MORE LOOSELY, "WE'RE NUMBER ONE."

WELL, THAT'S IT FOR TODAY, BOYS AND GIRLS! WE'VE BEEN CHATTING WITH ALUMNUS DR. ALI MAHDAVI ABOUT HIS WORK ON IRAN'S NEW ISLAMIC COURT!

DR. MAHDAVI WILL BE GOING FROM HERE TO HIS CLASS REUNION, WHERE YOURS TRULY WILL BE ONCE AGAIN TENDING BAR!

THANKS FOR BEING WITH US, DR. MAHDAVI. WE CERTAINLY WANT TO WISH YOU AND YOUR GOVERNMENT THE BEST OF LUCK WITH YOUR NEW EXPERIMENT IN HOLY FASCISM!

THANK YOU.

SO UNTIL TOMORROW, BUCKAROOS, THIS IS..

HOLY WHAT?

HOW DO YOU WANT YOUR COFFEE, MR. HALBERSTAM?

BLACK, JOANIE, VERY BLACK, UTTERLY WITHOUT CREAM AND SUGAR!

AS I TOLD JOANIE ON THE PHONE, I'VE ALWAYS WANTED TO MEET YOU, RICHARD RATHBONE REDFERN. DICK. EVERYONE CALLS YOU DICK, RIGHT?

NO, RICK.

WHATEVER, YOU'RE AN AWESOME FIGURE ON THE LANDSCAPE, BIG, VERY BIG, ONE OF THE STAGGERING SUCCESS STORIES OF OUR BUSINESS...

JOANIE, I THINK YOU SHOULD HEAR THIS.

SHE ALREADY KNOWS. HER INTUITION IS EXTRAORDINARY, ALMOST GOD-LIKE.

YOU KNOW, DICK, WHEN I THINK OF YOUR NEW YORK GLORY DAYS BACK ON THE OLD "TRIBUNE," IT JUST SENDS CHILLS UP MY SPINE.

THOSE WERE THE DAYS, ALL RIGHT.

WERE THEY EVER! I DON'T THINK I'LL EVER FORGET YOUR COLUMNS, HOW YOU USED TO FILL THEM WITH ANECDOTES..

THEY WERE BIG, GLISTENING ANECDOTES, VERY MOVING, VERY BRIGHT, ANECDOTES THAT PILED ONE UPON ANOTHER TO FORM A SPRAWLING MOSAIC OF OUR TIMES, THAT WAS HOW BRILLIANT THEY WERE.

OF COURSE, I WAS ONLY STAMPS EDITOR THEN.

NO MATTER. YOU OWNED THE TOWN.

OKAY, THAT BRINGS US UP TO THE LONG, HOT SUMMER OF '68. THAT'S WHEN YOU WERE SENT TO WASHINGTON TO COVER RESURRECTION CITY, RIGHT?

UM.. YEAH, THAT'S RIGHT..

AND IT WAS THERE THAT YOU BECAME SOMETHING OF A DEITY TO YOUR COLLEAGUES, THEY WERE IN AWE OF YOU, BUT THAT DID NOT LESSEN YOUR DEDICATION, IT INCREASED IT, RIGHT?

I JUST DIDN'T KNOW ANY OTHER WAY, DAVID.

OF COURSE, YOU DIDN'T. GOD, YOU LOVED YOUR WORK!

DAVID, BEFORE WE GO ON, I GOTTA ASK YOU—DO YOU REALLY BELIEVE IN THIS JOURNALIST-AS-STAR NONSENSE?

GOD, NO! IT'S THE WORST THING THAT CAN HAPPEN TO BOTH JOURNALISM AND THE PUBLIC!

BUT YOUR BOOKS ARE A MONUMENT TO JUST THAT ADULATION!

MAYBE. DEBATABLE. SUBJECT TO DEBATE. BUT I THINK I SEE YOUR POINT..

WHAT YOU'RE SAYING IS THAT THE CELEBRATION OF THE JOURNALIST IS CORRUPTING, THAT WHEN HE BECOMES BIGGER, MUCH BIGGER, THAN HIS STORY, IT DOES NOT HEIGHTEN HIS EFFECTIVENESS, IT DIMINISHES IT, RIGHT?

EXACTLY. TAKE WOODWARD AND BERNSTEIN..

GODS. I KISS THEIR GUCCIS.

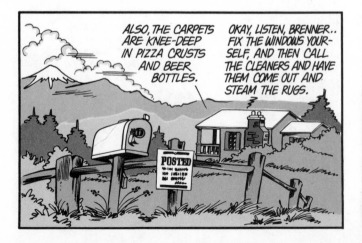

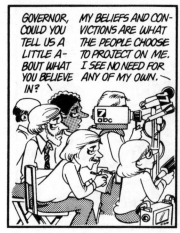

GOVERNOR, COULD YOU TELL US A LITTLE ABOUT WHAT YOU BELIEVE IN?

MY BELIEFS AND CONVICTIONS ARE WHAT THE PEOPLE CHOOSE TO PROJECT ON ME. I SEE NO NEED FOR ANY OF MY OWN...

BUT WITHOUT CONVICTIONS, HOW CAN YOU ADDRESS SOCIAL NEEDS?

THERE'S NO SUCH THING AS SOCIAL NEEDS. THERE ARE ONLY POLITICAL PRESSURES. I PROMISE TO RESPOND TO ALL OF THEM.

THE PROBLEM IS THIS: WE HAVE A LEADERSHIP CRISIS IN THE CONTROL TOWER OF SPACESHIP AMERICA. THE PEOPLE WANT A LEADER. A LEADER TODAY IS SOMEONE WHO WILL REPRESENT THEIR EVERY WHIM.

I THOUGHT THAT WAS A FOLLOWER.

THE LAST SHALL BE FIRST. THE FIRST SHALL TAKE NEW HAMPSHIRE.

YES, YOU..

GOVERNOR, FOR SYMBOLIC PURPOSES, YOU HAVE GONE TO SOME PAINS TO KEEP YOUR PRIVATE LIFE IN THE PUBLIC EYE..

VIRTUALLY NOBODY HASN'T HEARD THAT YOU DRIVE AN OLD PLYMOUTH, LIVE IN A SMALL APARTMENT, LIKE MEXICAN FOOD, BUDDHISM, BOB DYLAN, ETC., ETC.

MY QUESTION, GOVERNOR, IS HOW FAR ARE YOU WILLING TO GO IN TRANSFORMING YOUR PRIVATE LIFE INTO NOTHING BUT AN ONGOING PRESS RELEASE?

YOU WANT TO HANDLE THAT ONE, LINDA?

OH, WOW.. NO.

GOVERNOR BROWN, IF I MAY JUST FOLLOW UP ON THAT QUESTION ABOUT YOUR BOX OFFICE PRIORITIES..

WOULD YOU SAY THAT EVEN THE FUTURE OF YOUR RELATIONSHIP WITH MS. RONSTADT IS RESPONSIVE TO PUBLIC MOOD?

YES, OF COURSE. WHY GET MARRIED WHEN A RECENT POLL SHOWS THAT 90% OF CALIFORNIAN VOTERS COULD CARE LESS IF LINDA AND I GOT MARRIED OR NOT?

I'VE GOT A NEW ALBUM COMING OUT, THOUGH.

YES, IT ALL COULD CHANGE.

GOVERNOR, ARE YOU COMMITTED TO ANYTHING BEYOND THE PUBLIC MOOD? FOR INSTANCE, YOU NOW SUPPORT A BALANCED BUDGET, BUT LESS THAN A YEAR AGO, YOU BITTERLY OPPOSED PROP 13!

THAT WAS THEN, NOW IS NOW.

UH.. EXCUSE ME, SIR, BUT I'M FROM WASHINGTON. I DON'T KNOW ABOUT CALIFORNIA, BUT BACK EAST THAT WOULD BE A FATUOUS AND CYNICAL ANSWER. I WONDER IF YOU COULD DO BETTER.

EAST IS EAST, WEST IS WEST.

THANK YOU.

SOLDIERS OF MISFORTUNE

Q: Given the uncertainties of the long hostage crisis, wasn't writing about it fairly risky?

A: That's putting it mildly. The day after I finished the series on Reverend Sloan's visit to Teheran, the Desert One debacle broke. I had to kill the whole series, rewrite it, and submit it again after passions over the episode subsided. Strangely enough—considering some of the things I was writing about the students—a number of the strips got through to the hostages.[1] The Iranians had reached a conclusion very familiar to me: that there is no danger of finding anything of substance in the comics.

[1]On January 15, 1980, hostage William F. Keough, Jr., wrote home that "spirits of Americans can be lifted in many ways; thus, to my delight, Trudeau got the message through that the U.S. is very much aware of its citizens, now in their tenth week of imprisonment."

HI, BOSS. WHAT'S UP? — **RICK, I WANT YOU TO GET OVER TO THE HILL TODAY AND COVER THE LINKAGE HEARINGS.**

WHAT LINKAGE HEARINGS? — **YOU KNOW, JACKSON, CHURCH AND COMPANY. THEY'VE JUST FORMED A NEW TASK FORCE TO LINK SALT WITH A SOVIET PRESENCE IN CUBA.**

IT'S ALL VERY NOSTALGIC. THEY'VE EVEN NAMED IT AFTER KISSINGER'S OLD CODE NAME FOR THE MAYAGUEZ RESCUE.

GOOD MORNING, OPERATION MANHOOD, MAY I HELP YOU?

GOOD EVENING. TODAY "OPERATION MANHOOD" WENT INTO HIGH GEAR AS SENATORS CHURCH, JACKSON AND BAKER FORMALLY OPENED THEIR SPECIAL LINKAGE HEARINGS.

WAVING A PARCHMENT COPY OF THE MONROE DOCTRINE ABOVE HIS HEAD, JACKSON DEMANDED THAT THE PRESIDENT FACE DOWN THE SOVIETS "EYEBALL TO EYEBALL, LIKE A REAL MAN."

IN ANOTHER DEVELOPMENT, THE SENATORS ALSO PLEDGED TO INVESTIGATE NEW EVIDENCE LINKING RUSSIAN SABOTEURS WITH THE SINKING OF THE "MAINE."

FROM THE CHEAP SEATS ON CAPITOL HILL, THIS IS ROLAND HEDLEY, JR.

GENERAL, LET'S GET RIGHT DOWN TO BRASS TACKS! IS THE SOVIET UNION TURNING CUBA INTO A FORTRESS-STATE? — **WELL, THE EVIDENCE CERTAINLY SUGGESTS SO, SENATOR JACKSON.**

FOR INSTANCE, A RECENT SR-71 FLIGHT BROUGHT BACK SOME AERIAL PHOTOGRAPHS OF A CUBAN MILITARY SUPPLY DEPOT. ONE OF THE PHOTOGRAPHS REVEALED A SOVIET COMMISSARY OFFICER EXAMINING A REQUISITION FORM..

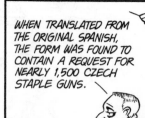

WHEN TRANSLATED FROM THE ORIGINAL SPANISH, THE FORM WAS FOUND TO CONTAIN A REQUEST FOR NEARLY 1,500 CZECH STAPLE GUNS.

STAPLE GUNS? WITH AN OFFENSIVE CAPABILITY? — **LET'S JUST SAY THE TECHNOLOGY IS AVAILABLE.**

GENERAL, IN YOUR OPINION, DOES THE PRESENCE OF THE SOVIET BRIGADE PRESENT A LEGITIMATE THREAT TO THE SECURITY OF THIS COUNTRY? — **SENATOR BAKER, I'D BE LESS THAN CANDID IF I DENIED IT.**

MY PERSONAL EVALUATION IS THAT THESE 3,000 RUSSIAN SHOCK TROOPS COULD BE EASILY DEPLOYED TO SPEARHEAD A MASSIVE AMPHIBIOUS ASSAULT AGAINST THE COASTLINES OF FLORIDA, ALABAMA AND SOME PARTS OF MISSISSIPPI.

HAVING ESTABLISHED THESE BEACHHEADS, THE SOVIETS WOULD THEN BE FREE TO FAN OUT ACROSS THE SOUTH, DISRUPTING TRAFFIC, AND EFFECTIVELY CRIPPLING THE TOURIST INDUSTRY SO VITAL TO THE ECONOMY OF THE REGION.

MY GOD! THINK OF THE JOBS! — **YES, SIR. AND THAT'S ONLY ONE SCENARIO.**

..AND TELL THOSE CLOWNS UP IN SACRAMENTO THAT JERRY'S **SERIOUS** ABOUT HIS PLANETARIUM APPROPRIATIONS BILL!

OKAY, I HEAR YOU.

ALSO, SEE THAT THE DRIVER PICKS UP THE GOVERNOR AT 6:30 TO TAKE HIM TO THE ANTI-NUKE CLAM BAKE.

GOT IT. ANYTHING ELSE?

YES. DO YOU KNOW IF SKYLAB HAS LANDED YET?

NOT SURE. WHY?

JERRY WOULD LIKE TO BE THERE TO MEET IT.

OKAY. I'LL PUT OUT SOME FEELERS.

SYMBOLS. DELACOURT HERE.

HI, DUANE, IT'S GRAY. WE'VE GOT A PROBLEM.

NBC HAS BROKEN A STORY THAT'S GIVING US SOME P.R. HEADACHES. THEY'RE CLAIMING THAT JERRY ONCE SOLICITED A $1000 CONTRIBUTION FROM A LOCAL MAFIA BIGGIE.

WELL?

WELL, WHAT?

IS IT TRUE?

THAT'S NOT YOUR DEPARTMENT! I MEAN, OF **COURSE** NOT!

LET ME GET THIS STRAIGHT, GRAY— **WHO** EXACTLY DID JERRY SOLICIT THE CONTRIBUTION FROM?

A GUY NAMED SIDNEY KORSHAK. HE'S THE LOCAL LOW-LIFE, AN ALUMNUS FROM THE CAPONE MOB..

UNFORTUNATELY, IT DOESN'T STOP WITH THE CONTRIBUTION. JERRY ALSO TRIED TO CLOSE A RACE TRACK AS A FAVOR TO A STRIKING UNION. GUESS WHO WAS REPRESENTING THE UNION?

COULD BE A COINCIDENCE, RIGHT?

WELL, THAT'S UP TO YOU, DUANE. JERRY WANTS YOU TO WORK UP A P.R. STRATEGY AND MEET HIM AT EL ADOBE FOR DINNER.

GRAY, I DON'T "WORK UP P.R. STRATEGIES." I CREATE SYMBOLS.

SUIT YOURSELF. BUT HE'S GOING TO WANT TO SEE SOME LAYOUTS.

GRAY TELLS ME WE'VE GOT A BIT OF A PROBLEM, GOVERNOR.

YEAH, AND IT'S NOT FAIR. I DON'T EVEN **KNOW** THIS CREEP KORSHAK!

YOU DON'T?

OKAY, SO I MAY HAVE RUN INTO HIM A FEW TIMES AT LEW WASSERMAN'S PARTIES.

WHO?

LEW WASSERMAN. HE'S A MOVIE MOGUL. HE HAS TO DEAL WITH KORSHAK TO GET HIS MOVIES MADE.

MOVIES? GOVERNOR, WHAT'S THAT GOT TO DO WITH..

LOOK, THAT'S ALL I KNOW. I WAS IN AFRICA. I'VE GOT WITNESSES.

GOVERNOR, IF I'M GO-ING TO HANDLE THE PRESS ON THIS ONE, I'M GOING TO NEED ALL THE INFORMATION YOU CAN GIVE ME.

NO PROBLEM. I HAVE NOTHING TO HIDE.

GOOD. NOW, WHEN THE NBC REPORTER ASKED YOU WHY YOU SOLICITED $1000 FROM A KNOWN ORGANIZED CRIME FIGURE, HOW EX-ACTLY DID YOU JUSTIFY IT?

I POINTED OUT THAT EVEN JANE FONDA HAD ONCE BEEN INVESTIGAT-ED BY THE F.B.I.

WHICH IS WHY YOU APPOINTED HER TO YOUR ARTS COMMIS-SION?

ABSOLUTELY. I BELIEVE THESE PEOPLE CAN BE REHABILITATED.

SO WHAT THEY'RE SAYING IS THAT I TRIED TO CLOSE A HORSE RACING TRACK AT THE BIDDING OF AN UNDISPUTED **MOBSTER!** ME, A FORMER **JESUIT**, FOR GOD'S SAKE!

IS IT TRUE, BOSS?

IS WHAT TRUE?

IS IT TRUE THE FIX WAS IN?

THEY MAKE A PRETTY FAIR TACO HERE, DON'T YOU THINK?

BOSS..

WHAT'S "AN UN-DISPUTED MOBSTER" REALLY MEAN, ANYWAY? ISN'T THAT JUST A TIRED CLICHÉ?

DUANE, THE BOSS IS REAL-LY STARTING TO FEEL THE HEAT, BUDDY.

I'M ON IT, GRAY. I CALLED A PRESS CONFERENCE FOR THIS AFTERNOON.

HOW ARE YOU PLANNING TO EXPLAIN JER-RY'S ASSOCI-ATION WITH KORSHAK?

WELL, I THOUGHT I'D SAY THAT BROWN IS INTRIGUED BY THE MAFIA ONLY AS A SOURCE OF IDEAS.

I'LL POINT OUT THAT ORGANIZED CRIME IS ONE OF THE FEW LABOR-INTENSIVE INDUSTRIES TO BE BOTH SELF-REGULATORY AND COST-EFFICIENT.

SO WE ALL HAVE MUCH TO LEARN, ETC.?

EXACTLY. I THOUGHT I'D SHOW SOME FLOW CHARTS.

UH.. ROLAND, IF YOU DON'T MIND, I'D LIKE TO GET THIS THING STARTED..

JUST ONE QUICK STAND-UP, BUDDY, AND WE'LL BE OUT OF YOUR WAY!

THIS IS ROLAND HEDLEY, JR., IN LOS ANGELES. TONIGHT, ABC NEWS LOOKS AT A SORDID STORY ABOUT THE TANGLED DESTINIES OF A GOVERNOR, A RACKETEER, AND A MOVIE TYCOON!

IT'S ALSO A STORY OF INFLUENCE AND FIXING, BUT HEY, LET'S LET THE GRAND JURY SORT **THAT** OUT! FOR NOW, LET'S LISTEN TO BROWN SPOKESMAN DUANE DELACOURT TRY TO DEFEND HIS BOSS!

UH..

THIRTY SECONDS, BUDDY.

ROLLING!

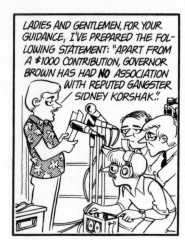
LADIES AND GENTLEMEN, FOR YOUR GUIDANCE, I'VE PREPARED THE FOLLOWING STATEMENT: "APART FROM A $1000 CONTRIBUTION, GOVERNOR BROWN HAS HAD **NO** ASSOCIATION WITH REPUTED GANGSTER SIDNEY KORSHAK."

EXCUSE ME, DUANE. IN 1974, THE RESTAURANT EMPLOYEES UNION GAVE BROWN OVER $50,000. KORSHAK'S CONNECTIONS WITH THE UNION ARE WELL-KNOWN.

OH..

YOU WANT ME TO FIX THAT ON YOUR COPIES?

NO, NO, WE CAN REMEMBER.

DUANE, HOW FAR BACK DOES JERRY GO WITH SIDNEY KORSHAK?

I ALREADY TOLD YOU! THEY BARELY KNOW EACH OTHER!

DID JERRY KNOW HIM WHEN HE WAS RUNNING WITH JAKE "GREASY THUMB" GUZIK, AL CAPONE'S OLD ACCOUNTANT?

"GREASY THUMB" GUZIK?

LADIES AND GENTLEMEN, BEFORE THIS GETS OUT OF CONTROL, MAY I JUST REMIND YOU THAT WE'RE TALKING ABOUT THE **GOVERNOR** OF THE STATE OF **CALIFORNIA!**

DUANE, DOES JERRY PACK A PIECE?

I DOUBT IT. HE'S PARTIAL TO SOFTWARE.

DUANE, SIDNEY KORSHAK HAS BEEN CHARACTERIZED BY THE JUSTICE DEPARTMENT AS ONE OF THE MOST POWERFUL UNDERWORLD FIGURES IN THE COUNTRY.

AND YET JERRY BROWN PARTIES WITH HIM, AND MOVIE MOGULS LIKE MCA'S LEW WASSERMAN AND PARAMOUNT'S ROBERT EVANS ARE CLOSE, PERSONAL FRIENDS OF HIS.

EVEN JERRY'S FATHER, PAT BROWN, LUNCHES WITH HIM REGULARLY. DUANE, COULD YOU EXPLAIN SIDNEY KORSHAK'S MAGIC?

HIS MAGIC EMERGES. HE VIEWS THE STATUTE OF LIMITATIONS AS A PROCESS.

I'LL BET.

FOR THE **LAST** TIME, GOVERNOR BROWN HAS **NEVER..**

THAT WAS THE VOICE OF PROTEST FROM THE BROWN CAMP HERE TODAY!

TOP FLACK DUANE DELACOURT PROVED ADAMANT IN HIS DENIAL OF ANY BROWN WRONGDOING IN A SCHEME TO HELP RACKETEER SIDNEY KORSHAK'S RACE TRACK UNION!

BUT ABC NEWS HAS LEARNED THAT BROWN WAS SEEN LUNCHING AT "THE BISTRO," KORSHAK'S RESTAURANT, THE SAME DAY HE MOVED TO CLOSE THE TRACK!

NOW, WAIT JUST A **MINUTE,** ROLAND..

BROWN WAS SAID TO HAVE HAD THE DUCK.

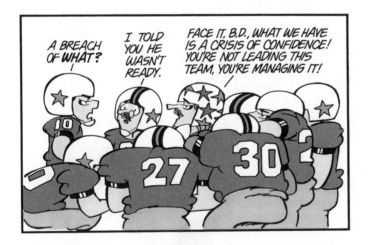

DUKE? DUKE, ARE YOU OKAY? IT'S ME, BRENNER!

BRENNER? BRENNER, MY MAN-SERVANT?

BRENNER, YOUR CARETAKER. WHAT ARE YOU DOING DOWN THERE, MAN?

CELEBRATING. I'M OFF WELFARE. I CAN AFFORD YOU NOW.

THAT'S GOOD NEWS, MAN. WHAT'S THE JOB?

IT'S CONFIDENTIAL, BRENNER. IN FACT, IT'S SO SENSITIVE, SO CRITICAL, EVEN I DON'T KNOW WHAT IT IS! AS OF TODAY YOU'RE WORKING FOR A MAN ON THE CUTTING EDGE OF HISTORY!

SOUNDS DICEY, MAN. I'LL NEED A DEPOSIT.

BRENNER, YOU JUST WROTE YOURSELF OUT OF MY MEMOIRS.

LOOK, DUKE, BEFORE YOU GO, WE HAVE TO TALK ABOUT FINANCES. I HAVEN'T BEEN PAID IN A YEAR!

NEITHER HAVE I, BRENNER. WE ALL HAVE OUR CROSSES TO BEAR.

DUKE, I'M SERIOUS! IF YOU DON'T PAY ME NOW, I DON'T SEE HOW I'LL BE ABLE TO KEEP..

PAY YOU? PAY YOU FOR WHAT? YOU CALL YOURSELF A CARETAKER? LOOK AT THIS PLACE!

YOU DON'T UNDERSTAND, MAN. SEE, MY OL' LADY IS EXPECTING, AND..

DAMMIT, BRENNER! DON'T DRAG YOUR PERSONAL LIFE INTO THIS! IT'S UNPROFESSIONAL!

OH.. SORRY, MAN, I..

YOU DON'T SEE ME WHINING ABOUT MOTHER'S TUMOR, DO YOU?

YEAH?

DUKE? ANDREWS HERE. LISTEN VERY CAREFULLY. YOU'RE LEAVING TONIGHT FOR THE DENVER AIRPORT..

AT EXACTLY 11:30 P.M., GO TO THE PAY PHONE BEHIND THE AVIS COUNTER. ON THE THIRD RING, PICK UP THE RECEIVER AND ASK FOR "MOTHER"..

NOT SO FAST, BIG FELLAH! I'M NOT GOING ANYWHERE UNTIL I SEE AN ADVANCE! WHERE THE HELL ARE MY KRUGERRANDS?

NICE TRY, DUKE. YOUR GOLD WAS DELIVERED YESTERDAY. WE'VE GOT YOUR CARETAKER'S SIGNATURE.

WHOSE SIGNATURE?

LOOK, DUKE, IF YOU CAN'T KEEP YOUR OWN PEOPLE IN LINE, DON'T BLAME ME!

OKAY, BRENNER, DON'T EVEN BLINK.

DUKE! WHAT ARE YOU DOING, MAN? PUT THAT THING DOWN!

I'M ONLY GOING TO ASK YOU ONCE, BRENNER! WHERE THE HELL ARE MY KRUGERRANDS?

YOUR WHAT? I DON'T KNOW WHAT YOU'RE TALKING ABOUT, MAN!

DON'T GIVE ME THAT, FUZZ-FACE! WHERE'S THE BOX YOU SIGNED FOR YESTERDAY?

THE BOX? I PUT IT IN THE REFRIGERATOR.

THE REFRIGERATOR?

IT SAID "RUSH," MAN. I THOUGHT IT WAS YOUR FRUIT-OF-THE-MONTH CLUB.

SORRY, "MOTHER," NO WORD FROM "EAGLE" YET.

DAMN! THERE'S GOING TO BE HELL TO PAY AT THE NEXT BOARD MEETING FOR THIS!

IF THEY'VE GOT "EAGLE," WE'VE LOST "DIPSTICK," COMPROMISED OUR LIBYAN SPOT MARKET OPERATIVES, AND PROBABLY EXPOSED THE KUWAIT PAYOFFS! WE'RE STARING AT A MILLION BARREL SHORTFALL!

OH.

WHATEVER HAPPENED TO EXPLORATORY DRILLING?

TOO RISKY. YOU DON'T SUPPOSE "EAGLE" WAS TOO STONED TO PULL HIS CORD, DO YOU?

"MOTHER"! A CABLE FROM TEHERAN!

FINALLY! GIVE IT HERE!

"REGRET TO INFORM YOU EAGLE HAS BOMBED. DIPSTICK."

MOTHER OF ALLAH! THEY CAUGHT HIM ALREADY?

GOD HELP US ALL.

A TOURIST? WITH OVER $200,000 IN CASH?

SO I'M NOT KARL MALDEN. SUE ME.

MR. McMEEL? ANDREWS HERE. I'M AFRAID I HAVE BAD NEWS, SIR. "EAGLE" HAS BOMBED.

DAMN! YOU SURE?

YES, SIR. IF HE TALKS, IT COULD BE EMBARRASSING FOR THE COMPANY! THE WORD IS HE'LL BE TRIED AND EXECUTED IN THE MORNING.

MY GOD.. THAT'S TERRIBLE..

YES, SIR. HE WAS A GOOD FRIEND.

YOU GOT SOMEONE ELSE LINED UP?

YEAH, BUT I THINK WE OUGHTA WAIT A DECENT INTERVAL. AT LEAST UNTIL THE STOCK MARKET CLOSES.

GOOD EVENING. TODAY FORMER UNITED STATES AMBASSADOR DUKE WAS CAPTURED WHILE PARACHUTING INTO THE AHVAZ OIL FIELDS IN IRAN. ROLAND HEDLEY HAS DETAILS.

THE REVOLUTIONARY GOVERNMENT OF THE AYATOLLAH KHOMEINI ANNOUNCED TONIGHT THAT THE ONETIME WASHINGTON REDSKINS FIELD GENERAL WOULD BE TRIED AND CONVICTED OF HIGH CRIMES AGAINST GOD.

ALTHOUGH DUE PROCESS AS PRACTICED IN THE WEST IS VIRTUALLY UNKNOWN HERE, ABC NEWS HAS LEARNED THAT AMBASSADOR DUKE WAS PERMITTED THE CUSTOMARY PHONE CALL..

HEY, MAN, THOSE ARE THE BREAKS.

DAMMIT, BRENNER! I NEED THOSE KRUGERRANDS!

THIS IS ROLAND HEDLEY. IT'S A BLEAK, DARK MORNING HERE IN TEHERAN AS THE ESPIONAGE TRIAL OF FORMER AMBASSADOR DUKE GETS UNDER WAY!

IN THE NEW IRAN, THE ISLAMIC KANGAROO COURTS ARE CUSTOMARILY GAVELED TO ORDER AT AN UNGODLY 4:00 A.M.! TODAY SHOULD BE NO EXCEPTION.

TENSION HAS BEEN MOUNTING HERE ALL WEEK AS..

THE WHOLE WORLD IS *WATCHING!* THE WHOLE WORLD IS *WATCHING!*

AH, HERE COMES THE DEFENDANT NOW!

THE WHOLE.. >THUD!< & UNH!

THE REVOLUTIONARY TRIBUNAL WILL NOW COME TO ORDER! THE COURT WILL HEAR THE ISLAMIC REPUBLIC OF IRAN VS. AMBASSADOR DUKE!

BAM! BAM!

HAS THE STATE PREPARED ITS CASE?

WE HAVE, EXCELLENCY.

LOOKS IRONCLAD TO ME.

THANKS. SORRY ABOUT THE TYPOS.

NOW, WAIT A MINUTE!

"THE PEOPLE FURTHER CHARGE THAT MR. DUKE ENTERED THIS COUNTRY FOR THE EXPRESS PURPOSE OF ESPIONAGE AND BRIBERY."

WHAT IS THE DEFENSE OF THE ACCUSED?

HE MAINTAINS HE'S AN INNOCENT TOURIST.

IS THAT CORRECT, MR. DUKE?

MR. DUKE?

OH, SORRY, YOUR HONOR, I WAS JUST WRITING A FEW POSTCARDS.

THE DEFENDANT, AMBASSADOR DUKE, IS CHARGED HERE WITH HIGH CRIMES AGAINST GOD AND THE ISLAMIC REPUBLIC OF IRAN.

HE IS FURTHER ACCUSED OF ESPIONAGE, BRIBERY, ILLEGAL ENTRY AND POSSESSION OF DRUGS. THE PENALTY IN ALL CASES IS DEATH.

THE EVIDENCE IS OVERWHELMING. I FIND THE DEFENDANT GUILTY AS CHARGED!

WHAT? THE HELL I AM!

THE BAILIFF MAY FIRE WHEN READY.

OKAY, *OKAY!* I'M WILLING TO DEAL!

MR. DUKE WAS THEN DRAGGED SCREAMING AND KICKING TO THE GRAVEL ROOFTOP OF THE COURTHOUSE, A POPULAR SPOT IN RECENT MONTHS FOR DISCIPLINING FORMER SAVAK AGENTS.

AS YET, HOWEVER, THERE HAS BEEN NO OFFICIAL INDICATION THAT THE SENTENCE HAS BEEN CARRIED OUT. CERTAINLY THIS REPORTER HAS HEARD NO SHOTS, AND HE HAS KEPT HIS EARS PRICKED.

MOREOVER, THERE ARE NOW REPORTS THAT SENSITIVE NEGOTIATIONS MAY BE UNDER WAY IN A LAST-DITCH ATTEMPT TO SAVE THE FORMER AMBASSADOR'S LIFE.

$500,000! IN GOLD!

$250,000! AND THAT'S MY FINAL OFFER!

YES?

HI! IS MS. CAUCUS HOME?

NO, I'M SORRY, JOANIE'S ALREADY LEFT FOR WORK.

OH. MIND IF I USE YOUR PHONE TO CALL HER?

UH.. MAY I ASK WHO YOU ARE, MISS?

I'M HER DAUGHTER, JOAN, JR.

"JOAN, JR."?

YOU MUST BE MOM'S OLD MAN.

"JOAN, JR.?"

YEAH, CAN I COME IN? I'VE BEEN UP ALL NIGHT ON THE BUS..

UH.. ARE YOU SURE THERE ISN'T SOME MISTAKE HERE, YOUNG LADY?

THIS IS JOANIE CAUCUS'S APARTMENT, RIGHT? WHO ARE YOU?

I'M A FRIEND OF HERS, RICK REDFERN.

GLAD TO MEET YOU, RICK. I TAKE IT MOM HASN'T TOLD YOU SHE HAS A DAUGHTER YET.

LOOK, DO YOU HAVE AN I.D. OR SOMETHING?

SURE. GEE, I HOPE I HAVEN'T SCREWED UP HER STRATEGY.

TELL ME, MISS, HOW LONG HAS IT BEEN SINCE YOU'VE SEEN JOANIE?

ALMOST SEVEN YEARS..

ALL THAT TIME SHE'S BEEN SENDING DADDY CHILD SUPPORT, BUT BASICALLY, SHE'S NEVER BEEN ABLE TO DEAL WITH THE FACT THAT SHE JUST SORT OF SPLIT ON US.

GEE, I.. I DON'T KNOW WHAT TO SAY, MISS. THIS IS SOMETHING OF A SHOCK..

PLEASE, CALL ME JOAN, JR.

RIGHT. I'LL NEED SOME TIME ON THAT ONE.

I UNDERSTAND. CAN I GET YOU A GLASS OF WATER?

GOOD EVENING. TODAY "TIME" MAGAZINE PUBLISHED PART II OF THE MOST TRUMPETED MEMOIRS IN HISTORY— "HENRY KISSINGER, THE WHITEWASH YEARS."

AFTER A SUMMER OF FAWNING KISSINGER STORIES, "TIME" HAS FINALLY ARRIVED AT THE MAIN EVENT—AN ORGY OF EXCERPTS FROM A BOOK "TIME" ITSELF WILL PUBLISH..

IS THIS HOW THE RULING CLASS PROMOTES ITS OWN? I'M ROLAND HEDLEY. STAY WITH US FOR A LOOK AT WHAT HAPPENS WHEN A NEWS-WEEKLY DECIDES TO.. HYPE HENRY!

"HYPE HENRY: MEMOIRS ON THE MAKE," BROUGHT TO YOU BY THE CHASE MANHATTAN BANK..

HENRY KISSINGER'S "THE WHITE-WASH YEARS" IS NO ORDINARY BOOK. NOR IS "TIME" PROMOTING IT LIKE ONE. BILL WOOTEN, "TIME" MARKETING DIRECTOR, EXPLAINS.

WELL, WE STARTED SLOW, OF COURSE. WE RAN THE USUAL SEMIANNUAL KISSINGER PROFILES, REPORTS ON THE WORK-IN-PROGRESS, A FEW MENTIONS IN OUR "PEOPLE" SECTION..

THEN THIS SUMMER, WE POURED IT ON! AN EXCLUSIVE INTERVIEW, A FOUR-PAGE COLOR SPREAD ON HIS SALT LECTURE, TWO PAGES ON HIS NATO SPEECH! I MEAN, WE PUFFED OL' HENRY FROM HERE TO SUNDAY!

DO ANY NEWS STORIES? UM..WE MIGHT HAVE. THAT'S NOT MY DEPARTMENT.

THE KISSINGER STORIES IN "TIME": LEGITIMATE COVERAGE OR ADEPT PROMOTION? WE ASKED HAMILTON LEFF, EDITOR OF THE MAGAZINE'S RESPECTED "NATION" SECTION..

MR. LEFF, IS IT TRUE THE PROMOTION DEPARTMENT ORCHESTRATED THE NONSTOP KISSINGER COVERAGE THIS SUMMER? YES, THAT'S RIGHT.

IT IS? THAT'S MY UNDERSTANDING.

AND THE "NATION" STAFF? WE HANDLED THE PROOF-READING.

WHY ARE HENRY GRUNWALD AND THE OTHER EDITORS OF "TIME" SO INFATUATED WITH KISSINGER? NEW YORK SOCIAL CRITIC IRV BELL EXPLAINS.

OKAY, LOOK, THE GUY'S CLEARLY A WAR CRIMINAL, BUT WHEN YOU TALK ABOUT NAMES LIKE KISSINGER OR ROCKEFELLER OR BUNDY, YOU'RE TALKING INNER CIRCLE.

AT THAT LEVEL, THE FACT OF POWER AND ITS EFFECTIVE USE MEAN MUCH MORE THAN MERE MORAL CONSIDERATIONS. THE HEIRS OF HENRY LUCE UNDERSTAND THAT.

IS THERE ANYTHING THE AVERAGE GUY CAN DO ABOUT IT? SURE. SPEAK OUT. CRASH THEIR DINNER PARTIES. ANYTHING TO KEEP THE PRESSURE ON.

POLITICAL MEMOIRS ARE NOTORIOUSLY SELF-SERVING, AND "WHITEWASH YEARS" IS NO EXCEPTION. SO IS THE BOOK OF ANY HISTORICAL VALUE? WE ASKED HISTORIAN LEO PARTCH.

WELL, IT'S HARD TO TELL, REALLY, BECAUSE THERE'S SO LITTLE IN THE LITERATURE TO WEIGH IT AGAINST.

SO FAR THE ONLY BOOKS ON KISSINGER HAVE BEEN WRITTEN BY OBSEQUIOUS T.V. CORRESPONDENTS WHO STILL TREMBLE AT THE HONOR OF ADDRESSING HIM BY HIS FIRST NAME.

FOR THE RECORD, THIS REPORTER HAS NEVER ENJOYED "HENRY" PRIVILEGES. BACK AFTER THIS.

AND SO THE BIG QUESTION AT TIME, INC., IS THIS: WILL SURVIVORS OF THE NIXON-KISSINGER ERA ACTUALLY BE TEMPTED TO PAY MONEY TO RELIVE IT?

700,000 WORDS. 1,521 PAGES. THE 30-MONTH OUTPUT OF KISSINGER'S HANDPICKED MEMOIR STAFF. BY ALMOST ANY STANDARD, "WHITEWASH YEARS" IS A VERY BIG BOOK!

GRANTED, HENRY KISSINGER HAD MUCH TO ANSWER FOR, BUT NEED SO MANY TREES HAVE DIED FOR THE CAUSE? MOST KISSINGER SCHOLARS THINK NOT.

HELL, IT ONLY TOOK ALBERT SPEER 520 PAGES..

THANK YOU, MR. WEINBURGER. ANY OTHER COMMENTS?

JOAN, JR?

HI! YOU MUST BE MY ROOMMATE, CHING!

ALL MY FRIENDS CALL ME HONEY.

PLEASED TO MEET YOU, HONEY. YOU CAN CALL ME J.J.

WELCOME TO COLLEGE, J.J.

THANK YOU.

I SUSPECT YOU WANT TO BE FILLED IN ON THE MEN SITUATION.

WELL, LET ME JUST GET RID OF THE PARENTS FIRST..

ANY WORD FROM YOUR BOYFRIEND YET, HONEY?

NO, AND I FEAR THE WORST.

I KNOW HE WOULDN'T WANT ME TO WORRY, BUT I CAN'T HELP IT. KHOMEINI'S PEOPLE ARE NOTHING BUT A GANG OF COMMON HOODLUMS!

KHOMEINI? WAIT A MINUTE! IS YOUR BOYFRIEND AMBASSADOR DUKE?

WE FELL IN LOVE IN THE EMBASSY COMPOUND. ALL OF PEKING WAS ABUZZ OVER IT..

WOW.. HOW ROMANTIC!

WE WERE TO BE MARRIED. I WAS GOING TO OPEN UP A LITTLE RESTAURANT IN DENVER.

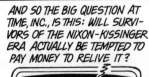

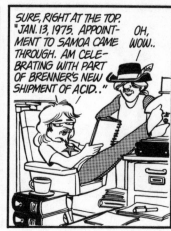

"APRIL 15, 1976. PEKING. INTENSE NEGOTIATIONS ON STATUS OF U.S./CHINA RELATIONS CONTINUE AT GREAT HALL OF THE PEOPLE.."

"TENG IS UNCOMPROMISING ON TAIWAN ISSUE. I MAKE NINE SEPARATE PROPOSALS, INCLUDING GENEROUS CASH SETTLEMENTS, PLUS POINTS. AM REBUKED AT EVERY TURN."

"APRIL 16. TENG REMAINS INTRACTABLE. IN ATTEMPT TO BREAK DEADLOCK, I CALL IN AIR STRIKES ON IMPERIAL PALACE."

"APRIL 17. PENTAGON OVERRULES STRIKES. AM LOSING FACE."

OKAY, IF EVERYONE HAS SOMETHING TO DRINK, I'D LIKE TO GET THIS SHOW ON THE ROAD.

I'M T.F. BANNON, COUNSEL FOR THE FIRM OF TORTS, TARTZ AND TORQUE, AND PERSONAL ATTORNEY FOR AMBASSADOR DUKE.

IT IS MY UNHAPPY TASK TO BE HERE TODAY TO READ THE WILL OF MR. DUKE, WHO IS.. UH.. PRESUMED DEAD AT THIS TIME.

STILL NO WORD FROM THE DECEASED YET, RIGHT?

NOT A PEEP, MAN. LET'S DO IT.

YOU A FRIEND OF THE FAMILY?

YOU MIGHT SAY THAT. I WORK FOR THE INTERNAL REVENUE SERVICE.

REALLY? HAVE YOU KNOWN DUKE LONG?

I WAS FIRST ASSIGNED TO HIS CASE IN 1963.

WOW..

HOW YOU BEARING UP?

NOT SO GOOD. IT'S SORT OF THE END OF AN ERA.

.."AND BEING OF ACCEPTABLY SOUND MIND AND WILL, I HEREBY LEAVE MY ENTIRE ESTATE TO.."

.."MY BELOVED PROTÉGÉ, MR. ZONKER HARRIS."

HUH?

OH, WOW..

YOU WERE HIS FAVORITE DEALER, I TAKE IT.

NO, NO, I'M AS SURPRISED AS YOU ARE!

YOU HEARD ME, PAL. PUT IT ALL IN ESCROW. NO ONE TOUCHES DUKE'S ESTATE UNTIL I SAY SO!

BUT, MR. HARRIS, WE'VE WORKED OUT A WHOLE INVESTMENT PROGRAM FOR YOU..

I'LL JUST BET YOU HAVE! WELL, YOU CAN FORGET IT! NOW, I HAVE A PLANE TO CATCH.

BE REASONABLE, MAN. WE COULD PUT YOUR MONEY TO WORK!

NO! AND THAT'S FINAL!

YOU'LL HAVE HIM DECLARED INSANE, OF COURSE.

CAN'T. THE JUDGE I USE IS ON VACATION.

GOOD EVENING. TODAY THE SMALL TOWN OF ROSEWATER, INDIANA, WAS HIT SUDDENLY BY A THREE-NETWORK MEDIA EVENT. IT WAS THE WORST MEDIA EVENT IN RECENT MEMORY.

THERE HAD BEEN NO WARNING. WHEN THE TINY LOCAL REPUBLICAN CAUCUS CONVENED LAST NIGHT FOR ITS PRESIDENTIAL STRAW POLL, ONLY LIGHT COVERAGE HAD BEEN FORECASTED..

BUT BEFORE IT WAS OVER, THE UNSUSPECTING TOWN WOULD BE BUFFETED BY WAVE AFTER WAVE OF REPORTERS, ITS CITIZENS INTERVIEWED AGAIN AND AGAIN, LEAVING THEM DAZED AND FAMOUS. ROLAND HEDLEY HAS DETAILS.

PEOPLE WERE JUST SITTING DOWN TO DINNER WHEN WALTER CRONKITE'S LIMOUSINE GLIDED UP TO RAY'S TACKLE SHOP..

THIS IS ROLAND HEDLEY. IT WAS SHORTLY AFTER DUSK WHEN THE MEDIA EVENT FIRST SWEPT THROUGH THE SMALL HOOSIER HAMLET OF ROSEWATER..

MEMBERS OF THE ROSEWATER G.O.P. CAUCUS HAD JUST CAST THE FIRST BALLOT IN A PRESIDENTIAL STRAW POLL. CAUCUS MEMBER AL FENDER EXPLAINS WHAT HAPPENED NEXT.

IT WAS AWFUL. THE HOT LIGHTS, THE CAMERAS. SOME OF US TRIED TO STAY OFF THE RECORD, BUT IT WAS HOPELESS. WE WERE FORCED TO STAND BY HELPLESSLY AS OUR REMARKS WERE BLOWN ALL OUT OF PROPORTION!

AND THE POLL RESULTS?

STRIPPED OF THEIR CONTEXT! RIGHT THERE IN FRONT OF OUR FAMILIES!

A MEDIA EVENT. UNTIL LAST NIGHT, FOR THE PEOPLE OF ROSEWATER IT HAD ONLY BEEN AN EXPRESSION. VICTIMS RAY AND ELLEN McNEIL RECALL THEIR NIGHTMARE.

I GUESS IT STARTED RIGHT AFTER THE CAUCUS VOTE. THE FAMILY HAD PICKED ME UP AT THE VFW HALL, AND WE WALKED THE FEW BLOCKS HOME..

AS WE GOT TO THE FRONT YARD, I SEE THIS FELLER IN A SAFARI-TYPE JACKET RUNNING AT US. HE WAS YELLING AND WAVING AND KEPT TRIPPING OVER THIS LONG, PURPLE SCARF. IT WAS GERALDO RIVERA.

"GET THE KIDS INSIDE," I SHOUTED TO ELLEN..

WE WERE SCARED. WE'D SEEN WHAT HE'D DONE TO ELVIS'S DOCTOR.

FOR THE CITIZENS OF ROSEWATER, THE MEDIA EVENT IS OVER. BUT THE SCARS LINGER ON. CAUCUS MEMBER SHELLY SIMMS SHARES HER TRAUMA AND SHAME.

WELL, I WAS JUST LEAVING THE VFW HALL WHEN I FIRST SAW THEM. I TRIED TO FLEE, BUT THERE WERE TOO MANY OF THEM. A BIG ONE, WITH A MICROPHONE, CORNERED ME..

I TRIED TO RESIST, I TRIED TO TELL HIM IT WAS JUST A STRAW POLL, THAT IT DIDN'T MEAN ANYTHING, BUT HE..HE..

HE WHAT, MS. SIMMS?

HE INTERVIEWED ME! REPEATEDLY!

WHO, MS. SIMMS? WHO DID THIS TO YOU? WAS IT ROGER MUDD?

NOW THAT THE MEDIA CIRCUS HAS LEFT TOWN, THE VICTIMS OF THIS SENSELESS, MINDLESS COVERAGE MUST TRY TO PICK UP THE PIECES. HOMEMAKER DOTTY HOLMES TALKS OF HER DESPAIR.

IT'S HARDEST ON MY THREE KIDS. THEY'RE HEARTBROKEN. THEY KEEP ASKING ME, "MOMMY, WHEN ARE THE T.V. PEOPLE COMING BACK?"

I DON'T KNOW WHAT WE'LL DO. ABC NEWS PROMISED US THERE'D BE A FOLLOW-UP STORY, BUT WE DON'T HAVE MUCH HOPE THAT ANYTHING WILL COME OF IT..

THIS IS THE FOLLOW-UP STORY, MRS. HOLMES.

OH. WELL, IT'S JUST NOT THE SAME.

HELLO?

HELLO, MS. CAUCUS? THIS IS MS. HUAN, J.J.'S ROOMMATE..

WHY, YES, HOW ARE YOU, DEAR?

FINE, THANKS. J.J. ASKED ME TO CALL YOU AND TELL YOU SHE JUST LEFT FOR YOUR PLACE..

SHE HAS TO MEET HER BOYFRIEND ZEKE AT THE AIRPORT, THOUGH, SO SHE'LL ONLY HAVE ABOUT TEN MINUTES FOR DINNER..

WELL, WE'LL CERTAINLY BE LOOKING FORWARD TO THAT, DEAR.

SHE DOESN'T WANT ANYTHING FANCY. JUST A LIGHT SALAD.

HI, RICK. LOOK, I HAVE TO MEET ZEKE AT THE AIRPORT, SO I CAN'T STAY FOR VERY LONG..

IT'S PROBABLY JUST AS WELL. MOM'S BEEN ON MY CASE A LOT LATELY, WHICH I'M NOT SURE SHE'S ENTITLED TO. YOU GUYS HAVEN'T BEEN FIGHTING, HAVE YOU?

LISTEN, WHEN I BRING ZEKE BY AFTER DINNER, TRY NOT TO BE TOO JUDGMENTAL, OKAY? HE'S A LIBRA AND VERY SENSITIVE.

HI, JOAN. WON'T YOU COME IN?

OH, MOM! YOU'RE NOT SERVING MEAT!

A FOOTNOTE'S PROGRESS

Q: You have been accused by numerous political observers of aiding and abetting the Anderson campaign. How do you plead?

A: Puzzlement. Anyone dumb enough to get his political information from a comic strip deserves what he gets at the polls. The Anderson strips were perceived as kindly, and thus an endorsement. The candidate's own view of the cartoon connection changed from week to week. At first he was disturbed, then he started quoting the strip in every speech. Later, both he and his campaign manager repudiated it.[1] It made it very hard for the public to keep abreast of the impact I was supposed to be having. In the end, I think I only swayed about three or four million votes, although which way I can't be sure.

[1]Anderson's final assessment: "I don't regard *Doonesbury* as the apotheosis of what the John Anderson campaign is all about."

GOVERNOR, YOU TALK ABOUT NOT LETTING OUR- SELVES BE VICTIMIZED. HOW CAN WE AVOID IT WHEN OUR STREETS AREN'T SAFE TO WALK ON?

GOOD QUESTION, MR. ANDREWS. HOW **CAN** WE AVOID IT? WELL, WE COULD BEGIN BY MAKIN' DARN SURE THE CRIM- INAL ELEMENTS AREN'T ON THE STREETS IN THE FIRST PLACE!

YOU TAKE YOUR WOULD-BE MUGGER. JUST HOW DE- TERRED DO YOU FIGURE HE IS BY THE THREAT OF A SUSPENDED SENTENCE?

NOT AT ALL.

RIGHT. NOW, SAY HE KNEW HE'D BE ELEC- TROCUTED ON TELEVISION?

WELL, THAT WOULD DEPEND IN PART ON THE RATINGS, WOULDN'T IT?

HI, IT'S RICK. IS HE THERE YET?

UH-HUH. HE AND JOAN JUST ARRIVED.

SO WHAT'S HE LIKE?

WELL, HIS NAME IS ZEKE. ZEKE BRENNER. HE'S FROM ASPEN, COLORADO.

AND?

WELL, HE'S QUITE..QUITE SOMETHING.

I DON'T THINK SHE LIKES ME, MAN.

WHAT ARE YOU TALK- ING ABOUT? SHE **ADORES** YOU!

JOAN SAYS YOU'RE A CARE- TAKER, ZEKE. THAT MUST BE INTERESTING.

YEAH, IT IS, MAN.

A LOT OF PEOPLE DON'T APPRECIATE CUSTODIAL WORK, BUT IT'S REALLY VERY CHAL- LENGING. YOU GOTTA BE PRETTY SHARP, YOU KNOW?

I CAN IMAGINE. BUT DOES IT PAY WELL ENOUGH FOR YOU TO SUPPORT BOTH YOUR- SELF AND JOAN?

OH, WELL, I DEAL A LITTLE DOPE, TOO.

MOTHER! STOP BEING SO NOSEY!

SO HOW LONG HAVE YOU BEEN A CARETAKER, ZEKE?

I GUESS IT'S BEEN ABOUT THREE YEARS, MAN.

IS IT SOME- THING YOU'RE PURSUING AS A CAREER?

NO, NO, IT'S JUST TEMPORARY UNTIL THE RIGHT OPPORTUNITY COMES ALONG.

I GOT A GOOD JOB OFFER WORKIN' ON A CONSTRUCTION SITE IN DENVER RECENTLY, BUT, OF COURSE, I HAD TO TURN IT DOWN.

YOU HAD TO?

I'M TOO SENSITIVE, MAN.

ZEKE'S A LIBRA, MOM.

SENATOR KENNEDY, DO YOU AGREE WITH YOUR FELLOW CANDIDATES THAT THE PRESIDENT HAS MIS-HANDLED THE CRISIS IN AFGHANISTAN?

WELL, IN THIS MOMENT OF NATIONAL CRISIS, ANY SECOND-GUESSING THAT I.. ER..PERSONALLY, WITH RE-SPECT TO THE INTERESTS OF PEACE.

MOREOVER, WITH THE.. UH.. UNCHALLENGED SOVIET THREAT, THE.. ER..GRAIN EMBARGO WHICH..UH..AS FAR AS STRONG LEAD-ERSHIP IN THIS COUNTRY!

NOW, IN RESPECT TO THE..

A VERB, SENATOR, WE NEED A VERB!

GOVERNOR BROWN, DO YOU THINK PRESIDENT CARTER WAS RIGHT TO RULE OUT A MILITARY STRIKE TO FREE THE HOSTAGES IN TEHRAN?

ABSOLUTELY NOT. NO OPTION SHOULD EVER BE RULED OUT. ESPECIALLY IN THE FACE OF A SERIOUS THREAT TO THE VIABILITY OF STAR-SHIP AMERICA.

FOREIGN POLICY HAS TO BE VIEWED AS PROCESS. UNDER CERTAIN CIRCUM-STANCES, A MILITARY POSTURE SHOULD BE PER-MITTED TO EVOLVE.

WHAT SORT OF REACTION TIME ARE WE TALKING HERE, GOVERNOR?

WHATEVER FEELS RIGHT.

GENTLEMEN, ALL OF YOU HAVE BEEN EXTREMELY CRITICAL OF PRESIDENT CARTER'S ACTIONS, BUT NO ONE HAS SAID WHAT HE WOULD HAVE DONE DIFFERENTLY..

EACH OF YOU HAS IMPLIED THAT SOME SORT OF DIRECT MILITARY ACTION MIGHT HAVE BEEN IN ORDER. DOES ANYONE CARE TO GO ON THE RECORD AS ADVOCATING THAT? SENATOR BAKER?

MR. REDFERN, I'M AFRAID I CAN'T ANSWER THAT QUESTION. THIS TIME NEXT YEAR I EX-PECT TO BE PRESIDENT, AND I'D RATHER NOT TIP MY HAND TO THE SOVIETS.

SAME HERE.

ME, TOO.

SORRY. GOOD QUESTION, THOUGH.

THANKS.

HEY, MARCUS, GUESS WHAT I JUST HEARD ON THE RADIO! JOHN ANDERSON IS GIVING A MAJOR CAMPAIGN SPEECH ON CAMPUS TONIGHT!

I KNOW. MIKE JUST WENT IN TO SEE HIM.

HOW EXCITING! MAYBE WE SHOULD GO, TOO!

YOU LIKE ANDERSON?

UM.. I DON'T KNOW. WHO IS HE?

I'D LIKE TO THANK ALL OF YOU FOR TURNING OUT TONIGHT..

MONDAY NIGHTS ARE ALWAYS BAD, SIR. IT'S NOT YOUR FAULT.

ZONK? HI, IT'S MIKE. LISTEN, I'M DOWN AT THE BUS STATION..

CONGRESSMAN ANDERSON MISSED HIS BUS, SO I'M GOING TO DRIVE HIM UP TO CONCORD.

CONCORD? THAT'S FIVE HOURS!

I KNOW, BUT HE'S A GOOD GUY, AND HE NEEDS THE LIFT. ALSO, HE SAID I COULD ADVANCE FOR HIM IF I WANTED TO.

ADVANCE FOR HIM? WHAT DOES HE MEAN BY ADVANCE?

CONGRESSMAN? WHAT DO YOU MEAN BY ADVANCE?

IN MY CASE, IT MEANS YOU GET OUT OF THE CAR FIRST.

SO WHAT'S MICHAEL GOING TO DO ABOUT HIS COURSES?

I DON'T KNOW. I GUESS IT DEPENDS ON HOW LONG JOHN ANDERSON CAN KEEP HIS CAMPAIGN ALIVE.

IT'S PRETTY EXCITING, THOUGH, ISN'T IT? OUR MIKE, ADVANCING FOR A MAJOR POLITICAL CANDIDATE!

NEVER HEARD OF HIM.

HE'S NEVER HEARD OF YOU, EITHER. JUST READ IT, OKAY?

ANDERSON? I'VE NEVER HEARD OF HIM. ARE YOU SURE HE'S ON THE NEW HAMPSHIRE BALLOT?

YES, MA'AM. IN FACT, HE'S SPEAKING TONIGHT AT THE YMCA AT SIX O'CLOCK.

SIX O'CLOCK? WELL, LET ME JUST CHECK MY BOOK.. LET'S SEE.. I'M SUPPOSED TO MEET BAKER OVER AT THE VFW HALL.. THAT'S AT FOUR..

AND CONNALLY'S DUE TO DROP BY THE PLANT RIGHT AFTER THAT.. AND, WELL, I PROMISED THE BUSH WORKERS WE'D MEET THEIR MAN OVER DINNER..IT DOESN'T LOOK GOOD..

BUT, HEY, IF ANYTHING SHOULD OPEN UP..

YOU PEOPLE ARE SPOILED ROTTEN, YOU KNOW THAT?

I'M SORRY, I'VE NEVER HEARD OF JOHN ANDERSON. BESIDES, I'M PRETTY APOLITICAL.

LOOK, JUST READ HIS FLIER, OKAY? WHAT DO YOU HAVE TO LOSE?

>SIGH<..OKAY, IF YOU INSIST.. HMM.. HMM.. ..UH-HUH..

HMM..THAT MAKES SENSE..HMM, I NEVER THOUGHT OF IT THAT WAY.. YES.. RIGHT.. YES, YES, THAT'S SO TRUE! BOY, THAT'S TRUE!

MAN! I THINK I'LL QUIT MY JOB AND GO WORK FOR THIS GUY!

PRETTY PERSUASIVE, ISN'T HE?

CONGRESSMAN? THIS IS DANNY WATTLE. HE'D LIKE TO SIGN UP FOR THE CAMPAIGN!

I REALLY LIKED YOUR FLIER, SIR. DID YOU WRITE IT YOURSELF?

UH.. YES, I DID.

GREAT STUFF. THE LAYOUT WAS NICE, TOO. VERY EFFECTIVE GRAPHICS.

DO YOU THINK YOU COULD GIVE DAN YOUR CAMPAIGN SPEECH, SIR? I THINK HE'D ENJOY HEARING IT!

SPEECH? YOU'VE GOT A SPEECH, TOO?

WELL, I SUPPOSE I COULD SAY A FEW..

IT'S REALLY GOOD. I'VE HEARD IT.

BOY, IS THIS GREAT!

THANK YOU VERY MUCH FOR YOUR ATTENTION..

BRAVO! GREAT SPEECH! JUST SUPERB, SIR!

CLAP! CLAP!

I'M GOING TO HAVE TO CALL MY BROTHER-IN-LAW IN LACONIA. HE'S PRETTY APOLITICAL, TOO, BUT WHEN HE HEARS WHAT YOU HAVE TO SAY, I THINK HE'LL CHANGE HIS TUNE PDQ!

THEN, IF HE AND I BOTH TELL TWO MORE PEOPLE, AND THEN *THEY* TELL TWO PEOPLE EACH, ETC., WHY, THE PYRAMIDING EFFECT COULD PUT YOU IN BUSINESS!!

I THINK WE'VE GOT SOMETHING OF A GROUNDSWELL ON OUR HANDS, SIR.

I'M GOING TO GET ON THE HORN RIGHT NOW!

GOOD EVENING. TODAY THE FIRST MAJOR SCANDAL OF THE '80'S SWEPT THROUGH THE NATION'S CAPITAL LIKE A TIDAL WAVE. ROLAND HEDLEY WAS THERE.

THE NEWS HIT WASHINGTON LIKE A BOMBSHELL. CONGRESSIONAL INVESTIGATORS HAD LINKED ATTORNEY GENERAL BENJAMIN CIVILETTI TO THE LARGEST ENTRAPMENT SCANDAL IN U.S. HISTORY.

ALSO CHARGED THIS MORNING WERE FBI DIRECTOR WILLIAM WEBSTER AND SEVERAL FEDERAL AGENTS WHO ALLEGEDLY RAN THE ENTRAPMENT RING OUT OF A POSH WASHINGTON TOWN HOUSE.

A TEAM OF SEVEN CONGRESSMEN, WORKING WITH A U.S. SENATOR, IS SAID TO HAVE BROKEN THE RING.

THEY'RE CALLING IT "CONSCAM." SEVERAL CONGRESSMEN, POSING AS THEMSELVES, HAVE BROKEN WHAT IS THOUGHT TO BE THE LARGEST ENTRAPMENT RING IN FBI HISTORY.

IT ALL TOOK PLACE IN THIS EXPENSIVE BRICK WASHINGTON COLONIAL. IT WAS HERE THAT FBI AGENTS REPEATEDLY URGED LEGISLATORS TO BREAK THE LAW AGAINST THEIR WILL.

THE FULL SCOPE OF THE RING'S ACTIVITIES IS STILL UNKNOWN, BUT THE D.C. OPERATION IS THOUGHT TO BE ONLY PART OF A MASSIVE, NATIONWIDE SCHEME TO DISCREDIT AND SMEAR PROMINENT PUBLIC OFFICIALS.

FBI MOTIVES WERE UNCERTAIN. BACK AFTER THIS.

HOW DID THE LEGISLATORS GATHER ENOUGH EVIDENCE TO BUST UP THE FBI ENTRAPMENT RING? I ASKED ONE OF THE CONGRESSMEN INVOLVED..

PIECE OF CAKE, REALLY. I SIMPLY PUT OUT THE WORD I WAS OPEN TO A BRIBE. THE RUSE WORKED LIKE A CHARM. WITHIN DAYS, I WAS BEING HANDED $50,000 IN TAXPAYERS' MONEY!

IN THE WEEKS THAT FOLLOWED, THE SCOPE OF MY INVESTIGATION WIDENED. TO MY SHOCK, I WAS OFFERED BRIBES BY AGENTS IN NEW JERSEY, NEW YORK, FLORIDA, EVEN TEXAS!

CONGRESSMAN, DID YOU FIND ANY HONEST FBI AGENTS? ONLY ONE. BUT HE WAS GREAT. HE WOULDN'T GIVE ME A DIME.

IF THIS SCANDAL HAS A HERO, THEN SURELY IT IS ARMSTRONG ALGER, THE ONLY FBI AGENT TO REFUSE TO ENTRAP AN UNDERCOVER CONGRESSMAN. ALGER DESCRIBED THE ENCOUNTER TO ABC NEWS.

ACTUALLY IT WAS VERY BRIEF. HE SIMPLY TURNED UP AT THE HOUSE ONE NIGHT, SAID HE HAD HEARD ABOUT THE BRIBES AND WANTED A PIECE OF THE ACTION.

I REPLIED IT WAS UNETHICAL FOR ME TO ENTICE HIM INTO COMMITTING A CRIME HE WOULDN'T NORMALLY CONSIDER. THEN HE BECAME MAD AND STOMPED OUT OF THE HOUSE.

SO YOU DIDN'T GIVE HIM ANY MONEY AT ALL? HE JUST WASN'T PREDISPOSED ENOUGH. LATER, HE CALLED TO CONGRATULATE ME.

WHAT WAS IT LIKE LIVING NEXT DOOR TO AN FBI ENTRAPMENT RING? NEIGHBOR WILBER FILBIS TALKED TO ABC WIDE WORLD OF NEWS ABOUT HIS ORDEAL..

LISTEN, I GOT THREE KIDS. IT'S HARD ENOUGH KEEPING THEM AWAY FROM PUSHERS AT THE PLAYGROUND WITHOUT HAVING TO WORRY ABOUT WHITE COLLAR CRIME NEXT DOOR!

IT'S SORT OF CREEPY, Y'KNOW? JUST KNOWING THAT RIGHT ACROSS THE STREET, PEOPLE WERE BEING INDUCED TO COMMIT CRIMES WITHOUT ANY PREDISPOSITION AT ALL!

EVER HEAR ANY SCREAMS? NO, BUT WE KNEW THEY WERE BAD NEWS. THEY ALL CARRIED GUNS AND NEVER CAME TO BLOCK PARTIES.

FOR THE SPECIAL TEAM OF INVESTIGATING CONGRESSMEN, OPERATION "CONSCAM" IS OVER. ITS MISSION HAS BEEN COMPLETED.

BUT FOR ATTORNEY GENERAL BENJAMIN CIVILETTI AND THE SCORES OF FBI OFFICIALS IMPLICATED IN THE ENTRAPMENT SCANDAL, THE NIGHTMARE HAS JUST BEGUN.

TODAY AS HEARINGS GOT UNDER WAY, CONGRESSMEN CAME FORWARD ONE BY ONE TO TELL HORROR STORIES OF BEING WANTONLY HOUNDED INTO ACCEPTING MONEY THEY WANTED NO PART OF.

COUNTER-CHARGES THAT THEY TOOK THE BRIBES WILLINGLY ARE BEING LAUGHED OFF. THIS IS ROLAND HEDLEY.

THE POINT I WANT TO MAKE HERE IS THAT I THINK IT'S TIME WE PUT BEHIND US THE DISCREDITED POLICIES OF FEDERAL HANDOUTS!

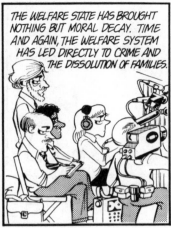

THE WELFARE STATE HAS BROUGHT NOTHING BUT MORAL DECAY. TIME AND AGAIN, THE WELFARE SYSTEM HAS LED DIRECTLY TO CRIME AND THE DISSOLUTION OF FAMILIES.

GOVERNOR REAGAN, DO YOU HAVE ANY EVIDENCE FOR SUCH A CLAIM?

CERTAINLY. I REFER YOU TO ONE REPORT I HAVE HERE FROM THE "NEW YORK DAILY NEWS" OF MAY 2, 1953..

1953?

"NAB WELFARE MOM IN BABY AXING.."

MR. REDFERN?

TAP! TAP!

YO.

YOU GAVE THE GOVERNOR A PRETTY HARD TIME TODAY ABOUT HIS FACTS. HE'D LIKE A CHANCE TO SHOW YOU WHERE HE GOT THEM.

TAP! TAP!

YOU MEAN, HE DIDN'T JUST MAKE THEM UP?

OF COURSE NOT. THEY'RE FROM HIS PERSONAL LIBRARY OF OVER 10,000 PRESS CLIPPINGS. HE'D LOVE YOU TO COME UP TO HIS SUITE AND SEE IT.

THE MAN TRAVELS WITH 10,000 PRESS CLIPPINGS?

WE KEEP 'EM IN SHOE BOXES. HIS CURATOR DOESN'T LIKE TO BREAK UP THE COLLECTION.

HIGGINS!

YEAH, BOSS?

WHERE THE HELL IS REDFERN? WE CLOSE IN AN HOUR, AND I DON'T HAVE HIS REAGAN PIECE!

HE CALLED IN TO SAY HE'S WORKING ON AN EXCLUSIVE, BOSS. REAGAN'S SHOWING HIM HIS CLIPPING COLLECTION.

HIS WHAT?

..AND THOSE ARE MY PRIZE "RED MENACE" CLIPS FROM "BOY'S LIFE"..

YOU CERTAINLY HAVE SOME BEAUTIES HERE, SIR.

SO YOU SEE, MR. REDFERN, WHEN I USE FACTS AND FIGURES, I'VE GOT THE DOCUMENTATION TO BACK THEM UP WITH.

WHAT YOU SEE IN FRONT OF YOU IS A LIFETIME OF CAREFUL RESEARCH. FROM "TV GUIDE" TO "READER'S DIGEST" TO THE LEADING AIRLINE MAGAZINES, I'VE LEFT NO PAGE UNTURNED.

THESE ARE MY "RIGHT TO LIFE" CLIPPINGS, OVER THERE IS "GUN CONTROL," "THE SOVIET THREAT," AND THE BOX YOU'VE GOT IS.. UH..

IT SAYS "LEAGUE OF NATIONS."

OH.. WELL, ACTUALLY, THAT ONE'S RETIRED.

"WILSON TO SIGN TREATY AT VERSAILLES." BOY, SURE TAKES YOU BACK, DOESN'T IT, SIR?

..AND WHILE IT'S TRUE THAT SOME OF MY CLIPPINGS FROM "LIBERTY" AND "COLLIER'S" ARE A BIT DATED, MOST OF THEM HAVE AS MUCH SIGNIFICANCE FOR US NOW AS THEY DID IN THE '30'S.

FOR EXAMPLE, DID YOU KNOW THIS? "STUDIES NOW SHOW THAT NEARLY 95% OF ALL PEOPLE ON THE PUBLIC DOLE ROUTINE-LY TURN DOWN HONEST WORK WHEN IT IS OFFERED TO THEM."

THAT'S VERY INTERESTING, GOVERNOR. YOU REALIZE, OF COURSE, THAT THAT'S UTTERLY PREPOSTEROUS.

I ONLY KNOW WHAT I READ.

YES, SIR. I THINK THAT'S WHAT'S GOT EVERYONE SO CONCERNED.

UM..OKAY, YOU GUYS ALL KNOW ME. I'M BROOKS HARKNESS, PRESIDENT OF THE SIXTH FORM..

TODAY WE AT ST. GROTTLESEX PREP ARE PRIVILEGED TO WELCOME PRES-IDENTIAL CANDIDATE GEORGE BUSH, ANDOVER '42, AND YALE '48!

AMBASSADOR BUSH, IF I MAY, I'D LIKE TO ASK THE FIRST QUESTION..

FABULOUS! LET'S GET A DIALOGUE GOING HERE!

WHAT WOULD YOU DO TO MAKE GOVERNMENT LESS TACKY?

I'D DO LOADS! THIS IS A GREAT COUN-TRY! GOVERNMENT DOESN'T HAVE TO BE TACKY!

AMBASSADOR BUSH, HAS BEING A PREPPIE HURT YOUR CAREER?

ON THE CONTRARY! I'VE FOUND THAT WHEN GIVEN A CHOICE, PEOPLE ACTUALLY PREFER TO VOTE PREPPIE!

AND WHY NOT? WE'VE GOT THE TRACK RECORD! WHY, OUR GREAT BOARDING SCHOOLS AND IVY LEAGUE COLLEGES HAVE ALWAYS PRODUCED MORE THAN THEIR FAIR SHARE OF LEADERS!

THINK ABOUT IT! WHAT DID SUCH GREAT PRESIDENTS AS WOODROW WILSON, FRANKLIN ROOSEVELT AND JOHN KEN-NEDY ALL HAVE IN COMMON?

THEY ALL GOT US INTO WAR?

RIGHT! THESE SCHOOLS JUST DON'T TURN OUT SISSIES!

AMBASSADOR BUSH, DO YOU FAVOR FED-ERAL GUARANTEES ON SUMMER VACA-TION LOANS?

GOSH, YES!

I THINK WE HAVE A SERIOUS YOUTH PROBLEM IN THIS COUNTRY! ANY TIME YOU HAVE TOO MANY KIDS LAN-GUISHING AT OUR BADLY CONGESTED COUNTRY CLUBS, YOU HAVE AN EXPLOSIVE SITUATION!

I THINK EVERY YOUNG MAN OR WOMEN OVER 16 SHOULD BE REQUIRED TO SPEND AT LEAST TWO MONTHS SUMMERING IN EUROPE. I WOULD FAVOR THAT KIND OF PROGRAM.

WHAT IF THEY REFUSED TO GO?

I'D USE FORCE. AFTER CONSULT-ING WITH THE AFFECTED NATIONS, OF COURSE.

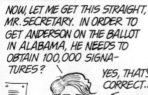

THE GERALD R. FORD PRO-AM SUMMER BI-ATHLON? WHAT IS A SUMMER BIATHLON, Z.?

IT'S A COMBINA-TION GOLF AND TAN-NING EVENT.

IT'S ONE OF THE MOST PRESTIGIOUS EVENTS OF ITS KIND. USUALLY, ONLY TOP LEISURE SPECIALISTS LIKE BRUCE JENNER ARE INVITED TO PARTICIPATE.

IN PAST YEARS, SOME OF THE TRULY LEGENDARY TANS HAVE BEEN SHOWCASED AT THE FORD BIATHLON — THE '67 SINATRA TAN, THE '73 CHER TAN, THE '77 ANDY WILLIAMS TAN..

YOU MEAN TANNISTS HAVE GOOD AND BAD YEARS?

SURE. EVEN THE BEST. HELL, GEORGE HAMIL-TON'S '63 TAN WAS A **HUGE** SCANDAL.

TELL ME, ZONK, HOW DID OUR FORMER PRESIDENT GET INTERESTED IN THE SUMMER BIATHLON IN THE FIRST PLACE?

WELL, ACCORDING TO THE TOURNAMENT PROGRAM, IT WAS ALL THE RESULT OF A RATHER HAPPY ACCIDENT..

MR. FORD WAS OUT ON THE LINKS ONE DAY WHEN HIS GOLF CART BROKE DOWN. HE DECIDED TO HOOF IT. AT THE END OF THE DAY, HE FOUND THAT NOT ONLY HAD HE SHOT 18 HOLES OF GOLF, BUT HE'D ALSO ACQUIRED A ROSY TAN!

AT THE SAME TIME?

IT WAS SOMETHING OF A BREAK-THROUGH.

I THOUGHT YOU HAD TO TRAIN TODAY, ZONK.

I DO, BUT FIRST I HAVE TO DECIDE WHICH TAN TO GO WITH.

I'VE BEEN GOING THROUGH THE "COPPERTONE GUIDE TO GREAT TANS OF THE SOUTHWEST." SO FAR, I'VE GOT THEM NARROWED DOWN TO "GAUCHO GLOW" AND "ALAMO SUNSET."

"GAUCHO GLOW" IS DESCRIBED AS "ROBUST, FULL-BODIED, A MAN'S TAN, DEEP AND EXCITING." "ALAMO SUNSET" IS "UNPRETENTIOUS BUT TART, AN AMUSING LITTLE COUNTRY TAN."

AN AMUSING LITTLE COUN-TRY TAN?

DON'T LAUGH. IT SWEPT THE GOLD AND SIL-VER AT PHOENIX LAST YEAR.

MIKE, IF ANYONE CALLS, I'LL BE OUT BEHIND THE BARN WORKING ON MY SLICE AND TAN.

OKAY. WHICH TAN DID YOU DECIDE TO SHOOT FOR?

I SETTLED ON A NUMBER CALLED "FREEWAY BOLD." SONNY BONO SPORTED IT DURING HIS UPSET WIN AT THE '79 CHERYL TIEGS DESERT CLASSIC..

THE LITERATURE DESCRIBES IT AS "A FLASHY TROPICAL TAN, A PRE-CANCEROUS GLOW FAVORED BY THE PROS."

SOUNDS PROMISING.

YOU BET IT DOES. TAKE A LOOK AT THESE COL-OR SWATCHES.

HMM.. NOT BAD. BUT DON'T THEY ALWAYS TOUCH THEM UP IN THE BROCHURE?

WELL MET, PILGRIM.

HI, SCOT. WHAT'S SHAKIN'?

BIG NEWS. I'VE JUST RECEIVED PERMISSION FROM THE IRANIAN GOVERNMENT TO VISIT THE HOSTAGES.

NO KIDDING? HOW DID YOU SWING THAT?

MY RESUMÉ. APPARENTLY, IT JUST BLEW THEM AWAY— ESPECIALLY MY WORK FOR AMNESTY INTERNATIONAL AND THE ANTI-SHAH DEMONSTRATIONS I USED TO ORGANIZE.

MY ARREST RECORD, OF COURSE, SPOKE FOR ITSELF.

WELL, I KNEW THAT WOULD COME IN HANDY SOONER OR LATER.

SO WHAT EXACTLY ARE YOU PLANNING TO DO IN TEHRAN, SCOT?

WELL, MY MAIN MISSION IS TO VISIT THE HOSTAGES, OF COURSE, TO OFFER THEM COMFORT AND LET THEM KNOW THEY HAVEN'T BEEN FORGOTTEN.

ALSO, IF THE OPPORTUNITY ARISES, I WAS THINKING OF OVERPOWERING ONE OF THE GUARDS AND HOLDING OFF THE OTHERS UNTIL I COULD RADIO FOR ANOTHER RESCUE ATTEMPT.

BUT I DUNNO. PEOPLE MIGHT SEE THAT AS JUST A BIG EGO TRIP.

YEAH. YOU HAVE TO GUARD AGAINST THAT.

SO WHEN DO YOU THINK YOU'LL BE LEAVING FOR IRAN, SCOT?

AS SOON AS POSSIBLE, MIKE. I'M TRYING TO GET A FLIGHT OUT TOMORROW.

HAVE YOU RECEIVED ALL THE NECESSARY CLEARANCES TO VISIT THE HOSTAGES?

WELL, NOT YET, BUT THEY SHOULD BE FORTHCOMING.

I'VE BEEN ASSURED BY THE IRANIAN GOVERNMENT THAT GETTING PERMISSION FROM THE MILITANTS AND THE REVOLUTIONARY COUNCIL IS PRETTY MUCH ROUTINE.

YOU BEEN FOLLOWING THIS STORY CLOSELY, REV?

NO, WHY? THEY'RE NOT ABOUT TO RELEASE THEM, ARE THEY?

TAXI, SIR?

WHY, YES! CAN YOU TAKE ME INTO TEHRAN?

OF COURSE. WHERE'RE YOU GOING, SIR?

ROYAL TEHRAN HILTON.

YOU DO HAVE A WORK ORDER PERSONALLY SIGNED BY THE AYATOLLAH, DON'T YOU, SIR?

A WHAT?

OTHERWISE, I HAVE TO CALL IN THE FARE AND HAVE PARLIAMENT VOTE ON IT.

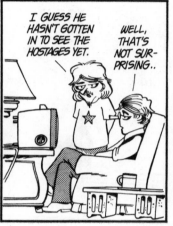

"AS TALESE EMERGED FROM HIS '57 TRIUMPH, HIS EYES LOOKED UP HUNGRILY AT THE FLICKERING RED NEON SIGN THAT READ 'LIVE NUDE COEDS'.."

"HE BOUNDED UP THE THREE FLIGHTS OF STEPS, ANXIOUS TO KEEP HIS APPOINTMENT WITH THE VOLUPTUOUS CHEMISTRY MAJOR WHOSE PHOTO HE HAD SELECTED WITH SUCH CARE FROM THE MASSAGE PARLOR PICTURE BOOK."

"WHEN THEY WERE FINALLY ALONE TALESE TURNED TO HER AND SAID, 'I WANT TO JOIN YOUR SILENT REVOLUTION OF THE SENSES, YOUR DEPARTURE FROM CONVENTIONALITY.' THE MASSEUSE SMILED AND REACHED FOR THE POWDER."

"MEANWHILE, OUT IN THE CAR, TALESE'S WIFE WAS GROWING IMPATIENT.."

UNDERSTANDABLY!

"IT WAS CLEAR TO TALESE THAT THE MASSAGE PARLOR WAS ON THE CUTTING EDGE OF THE NEW REVOLUTION.."

BUT YOU STILL HAVEN'T TOLD US WHAT THE BOOK'S ABOUT, MR. TALESE..

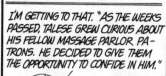
I'M GETTING TO THAT. "AS THE WEEKS PASSED, TALESE GREW CURIOUS ABOUT HIS FELLOW MASSAGE PARLOR PATRONS. HE DECIDED TO GIVE THEM THE OPPORTUNITY TO CONFIDE IN HIM."

"AFTER MONTHS OF SKILLFUL AND SENSITIVE INTERVIEWS, ONE OF THE CUSTOMERS FINALLY REVEALED THAT HE WAS MIDDLE-CLASS AND MARRIED. DAYS LATER, ANOTHER JOHN CONFESSED THAT HE, TOO, WAS MIDDLE-CLASS AND MARRIED."

"TALESE KNEW A TREND WHEN HE SAW ONE."

WOW.. I GUESS THAT'S THE ADVANTAGE OF BEING A REPORTER.

"NOTHING TALESE HAD EVER SEEN PREPARED HIM FOR THE EXPERIMENTS IN OPEN SEXUALITY HE WAS TO WITNESS THAT NIGHT AT THE SANDSTONE RETREAT.."

"ONLY A FEW FEET AWAY, SEXUAL PIONEERS WERE BREAKING NEW GROUND, PUSHING THE BOUNDARIES OF HONEST, OPEN COMMUNICATION BEYOND THE OUTER REACHES OF ACCEPTED SOCIAL BEHAVIOR."

"TALESE WENT UPSTAIRS WITH THREE OF HIS FELLOW REVOLUTIONARIES, AND FOR THE NEXT SEVERAL HOURS FLOUTED CONVENTION. SO PREOCCUPIED DID HE BECOME WITH HIS SILENT PROTEST AGAINST THE CENSORS AND CLERICS, HE FAILED TO HEAR A KNOCK."

"TALESE LOOKED UP TO SEE FOUR MORE PIONEERS."

HARDY STOCK, I HOPE.

HELLO?

REVEREND SLOAN? IT'S PRESIDENT BANI SADR.

YES, MR. PRESIDENT.

WE HAVE LOCATED THE HOSTAGES. DR. MAHDAVI WILL BE BY SHORTLY TO TAKE YOU TO THEM.

HELLO, REVEREND? DON'T LISTEN TO HIM! HE CAN'T DELIVER!

HEY! WHO'S THAT? IS THAT YOU, BEHESHTI?

HE DOESN'T HAVE THE AYATOLLAH'S EAR!

I DO, TOO! GET OFF THE LINE, YOU INSECT!

GBTrudeau